Reduced
to Equality

Reduced to Equality:

My Odyssey to Renounce Racial Privilege ~ and Find Myself

REBECCA HENSLEY

committed2change
unlimited

Author photograph: Crystal Boatenreiter
Book layout and cover design: Pattie Steib

ISBN: 1517558646
ISBN-13: 978-1517558642

Printed in the United States of America

10 9 8 7 6 5 4 3 2 1
First Edition, April 2016

DEDICATION

For R----- ~
who wouldn't be forgotten

and

For Morgan~
who told me
in no uncertain terms
that no amount of bullshit liberal guilt
trying to make apologies
will ever be enough

ACKNOWLEDGEMENTS

When you write a book and then sit on it like a dinosaur's egg for a considerable period of time — for whatever reason — it's hard to know who belongs in the acknowledgements. This is particularly true of a book about your own life since a number of the people who've played important roles in the amalgam of your days appear in these pages already and probably deserve to be thanked. Still, that would get to be burdensome at best and bizarre in some cases, especially related to those whose names have been changed to protect their privacy.

So I'll keep this simple. Thank you — again — to Dayne Sherman, who is just going to have to accept that I will be tipping my hat in his direction until I'm tired of doing so. His tutelage, his enthusiasm, his unfailing confidence in the potential of all around him who even *think* they want to write, and his friendship have made my life brighter, happier, and more productive.

My gratitude, as well, to Pattie Steib, whose skills, even temper, and professionalism made all the pieces come together as if it was easy, which I know full well wasn't true.

To my daughter's father (may he rest in peace). To my African-American students, who require on a daily basis that I boldly announce what even they wince at knowing. To the members of my family who will find this less than endearing and the new members I will come to meet because our story will finally be made public by one of us. Namaste.

And to all the people of color who have taught me the bulk of what I know about the socially constructed political notion of "race" and who only made me feel like an interloper when it was necessary to make a point: I offer my utmost respect and my undying commitment in the form of this book.

'Tis a gift to be simple
'Tis a gift to be free
'Tis a gift to come down
Where we ought to be
And when we find ourselves
In the place that's right
'Twill be in the valley
Of love and delight.

~19ᵗʰ Century Shaker Hymn

INTRODUCTION

He was small, even for ten. His hair was curly and a little longer than the other boys. He wore a baggy, striped t-shirt and baggy, rolled-up pants, decades before such garb was considered a fashion statement. And he was chocolate brown. But what I remember most about Reggie[i] was that he had huge, round, liquid-brown eyes with long, curling lashes, and he was wearing the biggest, whitest pair of men's dress shoes I had ever seen.

It wasn't just that they were white. They were dazzlingly, ridiculously white, having been lathered with flat, white sneaker polish. The strokes showed. The leather underneath was cracked with age and bore the shape of previous, much larger feet. Someone with great consideration had carefully made them as presentable as possible under the circumstances, but the shoes were so much too big for Reggie that they stuck out in front of him like big, flat, white clown feet. And his eyes wore the mark of knowing it.

As for me, I started every school year back then with two new school outfits, often, but not always, sewn by my mother, and one new pair of "school shoes," about a half size too big to allow for "growing room." Easter meant a new outfit for church, as well, and that included "Sunday shoes," often patent leather, to replace last year's pair. The older Sunday shoes — hardly worn over the course of the year, but by now pinching the toes — would then be handed down to a younger child or be relegated to a position of lesser importance, such as "play shoes." It didn't occur to me that a child might have more than two decent pairs of shoes at one time, or that a child should expect shoes to fit properly. But when I saw Reggie's big, flat men's dress shoes stretching out much too far in front of him on either side, I knew I was seeing something that I could not compute.

Now, the fact is that nobody I knew had much of anything in 1956. I had moved with my family — a father and mother, two younger sisters and a younger brother — from the mountain region of Kentucky to a working class suburb across the river from Louisville, and subsequently to northern Illinois by then. And while we had meat for most dinners by that time, we had started out originally without indoor plumbing and, frankly, I was still young enough not to be impressed by the difference.

Still, I had never recognized anyone in my tiny sphere as being what we called in Kentucky "dirt poor." Nor did I make the leap to define Reggie in this way. Rather, I compared him to the other boys and girls — both Negro and White (the terms we used then) — and seemed to understand that there was a variable missing in my conscious experience and that this variable was having some profound effect on this child's life.

"Dirt poor," I knew, meant having no shoes at all. But mountain kids, by and large, preferred not to wear shoes anyway and tried to avoid the practice as much as possible, even when they had shoes. No one I had seen since leaving the mountains was "dirt poor." In fact, walking through my neighborhood of big old two-story houses in a city that had been a city for more than 100 years, and going to a school that was built before the turn of the century, I felt as if God was in His Heaven and — as far as I could tell — everything was all right with the world.

Still, Reggie's shoes jumped out at me as if they had a life or voices of their own. They didn't just shout: "This kid is dirt poor." They mumbled: "This kid has no 'good' shoes of his own in a place where all of the other children have them." They intoned every time I looked at them, "What is different about this boy that he is wearing these shoes?" They didn't tell me that Reggie was different; they asked me why he was different and, at that time, I had no answer.

I'll never know what sort of feelings Reggie might have had about having to wear those shoes to school. I was not in his head. I was not a part of his secret world. I probably never spoke fifty words to the boy over the two years to follow before we parted ways to attend different junior high schools. And he most certainly did not speak fifty words to me. In fact, I don't recall hearing him speak fifty words to anyone during those years. But there was something in his eyes, actually a whole dialogue of sorts between him and me — a very light-skinned White girl with a Kentucky accent and a dark-skinned African-American boy in a pair of garish white shoes — that has continued ever since in my mind. This book is the product of that dialogue begun six decades ago. And this book is dedicated to him, as the first person of color to assist in the process of my broader education about the socially-constructed political notion of "race."

I refer to the concept of race as socially-constructed because I have since learned that it was more or less consciously created by White people in the 1500s to bolster a European desire to appear superior and to establish a position of dominance in the world. At that time, the newly established order of European quasi-scientists was encouraged by the historical needs of the moment to introduce a characteristic called "race" and then carefully define its categories so that one "race" was superior to the other. This concocted position of superiority was then used to justify the on-going social and economic exploitation of human beings who simultaneously looked different from and had resources coveted by European opportunists.

This so-called scientific stance would have been devastating enough for people of color as it was, but as the concept of "race" became entrenched throughout European society, the perceptions of superiority and inferiority began to appear to be not only normal, but natural. And, as European interests began to take over the world by brute force, it soon became completely reasonable to legislate matters pertaining to this "natural" phenomenon of "race." In fact, by 1748, when he drafted his seminal groundwork for a new and modern legal system in The Spirit of the Laws, the renowned French thinker Montesquieu, wrote: "It is hardly to be believed that God, who is a wise Being, should place a soul, especially a good soul, in such a black, ugly body... It is impossible for us to suppose these creatures to be men."[ii]

I knew nothing in 1956 of the social construction and political reinforcement of the concept of "race." And I don't recall having a conscious thought about Reggie or his shoes at the time, but I remember, to this day, concluding, as I looked him in the eye, that, in my estimation—as young as I was—there was something very wrong with a world where a ten-year-old boy would have to go to school wearing such a mark of dubious distinction. Precisely what was wrong and what could be done about it continues to command my attention to this day.

Perhaps, in a sense, he, intentionally or not, presented me with a bill that day, a bill that I did not accrue personally, but for which the circumstances of my birth made me, at least partially, responsible. Perhaps, instead, we looked across the great racial divide in 1956 and simply saw each other and acknowledged each other's humanity and made a quiet covenant (between cosmic—if not social—equals) never to let go of that moment until we stand in a new and different world, eyeball to eyeball once more, knowing that in some small way our covenant has helped to bring about the undoing of a centuries-old injustice.

---

[i] Some of the names in this book have been changed out of respect for the privacy of those who have played a part in my life, but might not want to appear in these pages. The use of the name "Reggie" represents such a change.

[ii] The Spirit of the Laws by Charles de Secondat, Baron of Montesquieu with the help of Claudine Guerin de Tencin, Book 15, Section 5 (1748)

PART ONE

1956

The massive hundred-year-old school made of dark brick sported a huge stone over the door that read "P.S. 101." Utterly intimidated, but with great resolve, I plodded slowly up the worn wooden steps and into the 5th grade classroom at Irving School, where thirty-five children and a six-foot tall teacher named Mrs. Walters faced the door at my entry. I was ten-years-old and wearing a plaid cotton dress with a black stitched-on apron, white bobbie socks, and brand new black and white saddle shoes. I probably looked incredibly prissy to the other students, at least half of whom were either middle-European immigrants or Black. And, in truth, when a little girl named Kathy stepped up and challenged me to a fight after school that afternoon, I simply snipped dryly, "A lady never fights," and strutted away from her, leaving a circle of startled and disappointed on-lookers as I proceeded homeward, my heart racing, without looking back.

Moving from an all-White, all-middle class, post-World War II suburban housing development near Louisville,

Kentucky, to the multi-racial, multi-cultural industrial city of Rock Island, Illinois, in 1956 was a monumental shift for a working class White girl. My father had become a professional man, it was true, college-educated through the G.I. Bill, and he wore a white shirt and tie when he went to work at the Headquarters, U.S. Weapons Command on Arsenal Island every day. But he and my mother and their four children were only a few brief years out of the mountains of Kentucky, and our move, upward mobility notwithstanding, restricted us to a "changing" neighborhood of big old two- and three-story homes bordered by cracked sidewalks and rough alleys.

It was not a bleak existence. Mrs. Math, a short, elderly woman with a heavy accent, ran an old-fashioned candy store on the corner, where it was possible to spend a dime for five minutes, and teen-aged boys wearing duck-tail haircuts played cards in a back room on the other side of a curtain door. Across the street from the store stretched a wonderful tree-filled park with a swimming pool, an ice skating rink, a summer day camp program, huge hills for breathless winter sledding, and tennis courts where dances were held for hormonal youth shuffling their sneakers bald on the concrete under the twinkling stars.

We played kick-the-can in the alley after supper until darkness settled around us and sent us home in answer to the calls of our respective mothers. We walked each other home from school, visited each other's houses, and played in each other's yards. I had a Jewish playmate named Sandra, whose family had shortened their name when they emigrated from Poland after the war. I had an Irish-Catholic playmate named Mary Ann, whose family ate fish sticks or macaroni and cheese every Friday night for dinner, which I found fascinating. And then there was Kathy in her glasses, who had challenged me to the fight, something that would never have happened in my old school. There were others, as well, from Europe and even some with accents, but my parents never said anything to me about the differences and I accepted my new classmates as equals immediately and without thought.

Even the presence of eight "Negro" boys in my class didn't impress me as remarkable. I look back now on this fact with curiosity. Why didn't it, I ask myself now, with all that I have come to know. Why didn't their presence amaze me or at least strike me as worthy of note? I only recall one previous encounter with a person of color which occurred at some distance as I rode by him in a car on a street in Louisville when I was maybe seven or eight-years-old. He was leaning against a brick building, I think, and had a sizable goiter on the left side of his neck. I still remember him, so he must have made some kind of impression on me, but I don't recall having any particular reaction to him at the time or afterward. I never asked and no one ever said anything about these "other" people, so different looking from me.

Many years later, when my son, Eli, was three-years-old, after the first time he spent a couple of hours in a nursery with other children, some of whom were African-American, I found him sitting thoughtfully on the back step behind our little three-room house.

"Does it hurt?" he asked me with concern on his face as I sat down beside him.

"Does what hurt?" I asked in return.

"Does their *skin* hurt?" he replied.

It took me a second to realize who he was referring to.

"Oh...you mean the *Black* children? Does **their** skin hurt?"

He nodded, still deadly serious.

"*No!*" I grinned reassuringly, glad I could give him an answer that would erase the troubled look on his face. "That's just the way God made them. God gave us this kind of skin and them that kind of skin, that's all. Like flowers in a garden — all different colors."

He exhaled strongly, visibly relieved, and jumped up to play.

When I was very small in Kentucky, I remember catching one of my uncles telling my mother in an excited voice the garish details of what must surely have been a lynching, though I didn't actually hear him say anything about race and he hushed as soon as he saw me. Another time, he said gleefully at the dinner table, "Well, the blacker the berry, the sweeter the juice, y' know!" And, again, my mother hushed him, shooting him a look of disapproval because of my presence. Apparently, at least some of the members of my family were racist, but they left me — at least consciously — a racial blank slate, as it were, and so, when I hit Irving School, I was allowed to concentrate on being the "new girl" and didn't give one thought that I recall to what it meant to be Black or White or Irish Catholic or a Jewish immigrant or whatever.

Still, the children in my fifth grade class at Irving put a human face on all those groups. It's interesting, now, to look back and realize that a few years after World War II, I actually played with Jewish friends who had doubtless left France or Poland or even Germany to escape nightmares, but at the time, they didn't speak of it and I was allowed to be oblivious. I did get to know my Catholic friend a little better, joining Friday night dinners as often as allowed, charmed by the idea of religious ritual. But, if I could go back, I would ask a lot of questions of all of my fifth grade friends, including and maybe especially, the Black ones.

The one African-American fifth grader I came to know best, though I hardly knew him well, was Jack. Jack was a good-looking, intelligent class leader with a strong personality and a ready grin, qualities that eventually, I learned much later, put him in a high-level executive position with a multi-national corporation. At the time, however, all that pizzazz was a little over-whelming to a new kid. Then, a few days after I arrived at the school, Mrs. Walters called on me to read aloud a paragraph about Louisville from a geography book. I was a good reader and not intimidated by the task, so I stood and read. Before I could even sit down, though, Jack raised his hand to make the point to Mrs. Walters and the class that I had read the word "Louisville" wrong because I had pronounced it "Lu-uh-vul."

Sputtering, I countered immediately, outraged, that I had just moved from there and that was the way it was pronounced by the natives (I had never heard of the "Lou-ey-ville Slugger" or that would have been a much better argument). He leaned over his desk, taunting me, and announced in a loud voice that I was in Rock Island, Illinois, now and that I should learn to pronounce it "Lou-is-ville" instead — the way it was written. I'm sure that he knew about the Louisville Slugger, but that wasn't the point. He was taking the opportunity to demonstrate his control over the situation in which we found ourselves. The class dissolved into laughter and I was mortified. Needless to say, I began the process of shedding my southern accent immediately. But that isn't the end of the story.

A couple of months later, Jack and I were chosen to be the focal point of a song for a school show. The song was "In the Good Old Summertime," and the costumes and ambiance were to reflect the turn of the century, so Mrs. Walters outlined her directions: I was to carry a parasol and take

Jack's arm, strolling with him across the stage while the class all sang. Still smarting under the humiliation of his open ridicule of me in the classroom, I refused to take his arm. Mrs. Walters was non-plussed, of course, since teachers in those days were not used to students refusing to do as they were told, but she did not ask for an explanation, as she probably should have. In any case, I was a bull-headed child and put up a fight, but I must have capitulated in the end because we wound up in a photo in the local newspaper in our costumes, arm in arm, like "Gone with the Wind" as it could only be produced "up north," as we used to say in Kentucky.

Decades later, I was standing in the back of a crowded room, listening to Jack, as an adult, give a Martin Luther King, Jr., Day speech about race relations and the pain of growing up Black in the 1950's. We hadn't had any contact for all those years and he had no reason to know that I was in the room, but I was surprised to hear him relate a story about how hurt he was when a racist little White girl named Becky refused to take his hand on a stage when he was ten-years-old because he was not White.

I approached him after his presentation, of course. We greeted and laughed about the amazing coincidence of my presence. I reminded him about the incident previous to my snubbing him when he ridiculed my reading, and he seemed to recall it, but I will never know whether he saw — or believed — the connection between the two events.

I did not mention that I was subsequently approached by some of his buddies who told me that he wanted me to "meet him in a closet," even though they volunteered the information at the same time that he already had a girlfriend — another White girl who went to a different school — and that, if I took him up on his offer, there would surely be trouble. I declined the invitation, puzzled as to why a boy would want to do such a thing if he already had a girlfriend. But memories paint their own history. It wouldn't seem that an African-American boy in those days would dare to invite a White girl he perceived as racist into a closet. Or perhaps they were only testing me, the way ten-year-olds will. Or perhaps he didn't send them at all.

The fact is that I never thought of Jack as other than a boy — a boy who scared me with his audacity and his power of personality, admittedly, but just a boy, nonetheless. His perception of how I saw him at that time, on the other hand, was driven largely, I must assume, by his experience of life as an African-American boy in a world where that meant infinitely more than I could possibly have realized at the time.

In my late thirties, I inadvertently met and spent nearly a year dating his younger brother and wondered once or twice what Jack must have thought about Marvin and I being a couple, but we never met again except the night I witnessed his presentation. It was all just as complicated as matters of "race" must always be in the United States of America at any time in its history to the present. This was typified particularly well by a comment I overheard my mother making to someone over the phone after the fifth grade concert: "I'm just worried that Becky is going to take up with a little boy named Jack from her class play at school. He's a Negro." My thought at the time was that, had she understood how I felt about Jack, she would have known better. But I found it odd, and even amusing, that she would care one way or the other. I now realize that what was odd — for a White girl in the U.S. in 1957 — was that I did not understand her concerns.

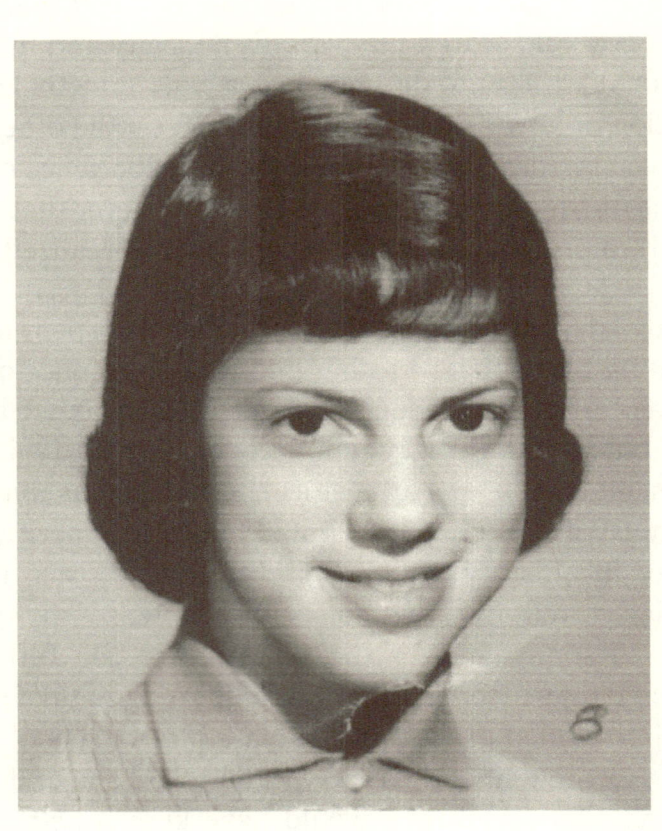

1959

At the end of my grade school years, I was promoted to Central Junior High School, where African-Americans and White Americans were joined by Latinos, most of whom were Mexican. There were Latino gangs, including girl gangs complete with over-sized jackets, and I had a crush for a while on Dick, a Mexican boy with a white spot in his hair, but was too shy to do anything about it.

Despite my unspoken angst over this particular young man, however, it was another boy who made me feel what I came to understand later was the visceral chemical response a woman feels when she's in the presence of a man to whom she is physically attracted. His name was Martin and he was a straight A student and a football player on the junior high varsity squad, dark and quiet, like deep water on a moonless night. I can only recall us saying hello to each other once or twice, but on those occasions when our eyes met, I became instantly quiet and sad. I cannot suggest why. Obviously, there isn't enough information available for me to know. But

I will always believe that, in a different world, I would have found out.

I eventually heard that he shattered somehow in his early twenties and, if that's true, I'm sorry. He must have been an anguished man and, knowing what I know now about the struggle of Black men in general, and very bright Black men, in particular, I am not surprised. He deserved better than he got. I don't know what it was that he got, but that he deserved better, I am sure.

I was not allowed to date until I was sixteen and the church my family attended prohibited dancing, going to movies, and playing cards, but every day at noon, after we rushed through our lunches, the tables in the cafeteria were pushed aside and students would dance to music from a juke box at one end of the room. I always danced. Most of the dancers were girls dancing a kind of cool jitter-bug with other girls, which was common in the late 1950's and early 1960's there. Few of the White boys knew how to dance, to speak of, and those who did may have been influenced not to bother by the lack of other boys on the floor. Then one day, DeVon, a short, light-skinned African-American boy with unapologetic eyes, walked across the floor and asked me to dance.

DeVon must have liked dancing because he did it very well. He led smoothly and with command and it was great fun to dance across the floor to "Stagger Lee" or "Alley Oop" with my fingertips held ever so lightly, but masterfully, by his. Looking back, I am astounded by his nerve. For a Black boy to ask a White girl to dance anywhere in the U.S. in broad daylight at school in 1959 was an act of huge daring. How did he know that I would dance with him? What made the risk worth doing? For that matter, what were the risks to him and did he ever wind up having to pay for taking them? I have no idea. We never spoke past, "Would you like to dance?" and "Yes." I only know that, at some point in the process, my best friend said to me privately one day, "You know they talk

about you because you dance with Negroes at lunch, don't you?"
I don't remember responding to her question, but I remember
wondering why anyone would care. Now I wonder why race did
not prescribe my behavior as it did theirs and, further, why I
didn't know — or care — how my choices would affect the
opinions of those around me.

Eventually, one of the Black kids came back from a visit
to the East Coast and introduced us all to "The Continental,"
a dance very similar to today's "Electric Slide." A group of
dancers would stand in a tight little clump, evenly space and
all facing the same direction, and they would move in perfect
synchronicity around the floor. I was mesmerized. I didn't
just want to learn this dance; I was compelled to learn it. It
took considerable time for me to master the little kick-step
so necessary to executing "The Continental," but I finally got
it and took the floor with the others, blissful in the motion,
filled with the music, one with the other dancers,
occasionally joined by one other White girl, but otherwise the
only White student on the floor.

It is only in long-distance retrospect I realize that this is
much like how I have spent my life, being allowed to join a
dance by people of color who are always more keenly aware
of my oddity than I am, but who, for the most part, either
welcome me, don't care, or are amused by my willfulness in
the face of those who find my actions so ignominious and,
sometimes, even threatening. But the music of human
history that refuses to consider how ready or not we are for
its latest developments, calls me to the dance and I cannot
stay seated. Still, I have often been made crucially aware that
there are those on both sides of the racial struggle who are
disgusted by my dancing. And I have paid more dearly than I
can ever completely communicate or comprehend for
answering the call to dance as I have done.

1963

In 1961, my family moved to Moline, an adjoining city, where I went to high school with three thousand other students, almost the entire population being White. I vaguely remember the "Anders boys," who were, as I recall, the resident football heroes, but other than them, I don't remember being aware of anybody in my world being African-American.

Certainly, the very large fundamentalist Christian church my family attended almost every day, had only White members. For that matter, when John F. Kennedy ran for President, leaflets in the back of our church promised that, if Kennedy was elected, the Pope would run our country. It was highly unlikely that someone who stood out at first glance even more than an Irish Catholic would find their way to our church and decide to worship there.

This reality makes my choice of social studies term paper topics in my junior year remarkable. In all fairness, I didn't come up with the topic myself. All the juniors at our high school had to complete two term papers, one in English and one in social studies. My English term paper had been on poetry written in the colonies before the Revolutionary War. I think I was late choosing my topic and it was the last one on the list or something. In any case, I did the paper, a massive commitment for me at the time, by spending interminable hours in the dusty back shelves of the library, poring over materials that were far enough out of the mainstream to ensure that having them in the dusty back shelves would be no particular inconvenience to the vast majority of the library patrons. Having finished that piece of work, I was desperate not to have to do another similar project.

"*Please!*" I begged Ann Steckal, my social studies teacher, "I can't do another month in the back of the library! Is there any way to do a research project other than that?"

Ann Steckal was young and she wore bright red lipstick and she grinned a lot and she was unintimidated by the classroom setting. Had she been more committed to the stodgy sort of teaching processes that resulted in some of my classmates dissecting carrots rather than frogs in biology class, her answer would unquestionably have been quite different.

"Well..." she began cautiously, "if you can get your parents' permission, you *could* do an all-interview term paper on 'Racial Discrimination in the Quad-Cities'."

Had she said that I could do an all-interview term paper on water polo, I would have jumped at the chance. The fact is that all I heard in that sentence was the term "all-interview."

"*Yes!*" I thought, rushing home to get permission. Actually, I had no idea what she was suggesting. I didn't know what studying racial discrimination would entail or even what it was, let alone how to interview anybody about it, should I want to, but if doing this project meant freedom from little index cards amid hours of brain-numbing silence, I was sold, regardless. It didn't occur to me what the greater implications were of a sixteen-year-old White girl trooping around Moline, Illinois, in 1962 talking to White adult authority figures about race.

I look back now and wonder where Ann Steckal is and what she's doing. Does she remember me after all these years? I wonder what she would think of my being a sociologist with a special interest in power relations, particularly concerning race. I wonder if she would smile at knowing how memories of her class have affected my own teaching style. I wonder what, in her own background or studies or interests pushed her to suggest the topic she did instead of any one of a hundred other, much "safer" possibilities. By my lights, I owe her a debt of gratitude. The bottom line is that she opened a door of opportunity for me that led into a psychic building I might otherwise never have known existed and I am grateful.

If she opened the door, however, it was Glenn Perkins who gave me the grand tour of the building. Perkins was the President of the Metro-Com NAACP at that time and had been a civil rights leader in the area for decades. In addition, as it happened, he worked in my father's office at the Rock Island Arsenal. After my father had given me his permission to do the term paper on racial discrimination, he spoke to Perkins and then took me to Perkins' home across the river in Davenport, Iowa, where the man graciously and most thoroughly prepared me for my first real sociological study.

I don't remember much of what he said that afternoon, but I know that my father and I were there in his living room for several hours and when we left, I carried with me six or seven type-written pages of questions carefully broken up into categories. One set of questions was for business managers; another set was for school principals. Other sets were to be asked of real estate agents or restaurant managers or barbers or ministers. Perkins had told me with clarity what sort of side-stepping to watch for and how to counter it.

"If a manager tells you that his store hires Negroes," Perkins instructed me, "ask him how many employees they have and what *percentage* of them are Negroes. Then, when he tells you *that,* ask him what they do — *specifically* — because you'll always find that they'll be stacking something, cleaning something, serving something, or pushing something around!" And he laughed.

Perkins was not a bitter man, though I don't know why not, under the circumstances of daily facing and dealing with institutionalized oppression in the name of racism. He was not a young man at that time and I have now been given to understand that he is no longer living. But I hope he knows that he created a monster of sorts that day. I really heard what he said, and I have used what he taught me that afternoon in executing literally hundreds of interviews for newspaper feature articles, sociological studies, therapy sessions with adult and adolescent offenders, and even my own fascinations ever since. He not only welcomed a teen-aged girl into his home on his day off, he took her seriously and armed her to be able to seek the truth in ways that have served her and her topics well for many years, ways that she would not fully understand until, as a highly trained professional, she came to call it "asking the right question."

I don't have a copy of the term paper, needless to say. Actually, the meat of it was only a few pages long, anyway, with a set of pages following wherein I listed the people I had interviewed and wrote a few notes about what I learned from each. But it got an A+, as I recall, and Miss Steckal asked me to do a class presentation on it.

Looking back, I realize for the first time that she wasn't just a great teacher, though she was that, but she may have been trying to make the world a better place, as well, and she was teaching me, at least, how to bravely explore human social reality. A well-known sociologist named Peter Berger[i] once wrote that the first wisdom of sociology is that things are not what they seem. Ann Steckal and Glenn Perkins knew that, and when they got done with me, I did, too.

I turned over a lot of rocks in my interviews, thanks to Perkins' list of questions. In fact, the savvy nature of the questions coupled with my presenting myself as if I was old enough to deserve respect from my interviewees (something that was not entirely true in 1962) caused many of them to go ahead and tell me the truth. Halfway through the session, they would lean toward me, lower their voices, and tell me "secrets." About bi-racial children being listed in public school records as "White" if their father was White and "Black" if their father was Black in spite of the fact that they had one parent of each race in both cases. About the fact that most employers in the area had only one or two African-American employees, but were quick to tell people that they "hired Negroes." About African-Americans being served at the best restaurant in town — on paper plates. Then, I went to visit the head of the local real estate board.

He had sold my parents their house, a run-down three-story classic in a "better" neighborhood, where some of our neighbors were downright rich and almost all were better-off than we were. It was a fixer-upper, for sure, but with the potential of being worth a great deal more than my parents had paid for it. He ushered me cordially into his office, showing me a chair and settling behind his desk with a patronizing smile on his face.

I must presume that I had told him what I was coming to talk with him about, but it may be that it didn't compute when I made the appointment, because as the questions continued, he began to resist. Finally, in a moment of fury, his face blazing, he jerked my notes out of my hand, scaring me half to death and lashed out with spittle flying, "Let me see what you're writing there! If any of this information gets past your teacher, your name'll be mud in the city of Moline!"

I was stunned. Not to mention terrified. I stood up, rescued my notes, and backed out the door. I was afraid he was going to attack me physically. All the way home, I was frantic. What if he could somehow take my parents' house away from them? And it would be all my fault!

My father chuckled as he assured me that our house was safe from tigers, and I proceeded to complete and type up my paper. The end result was that, at the end of the year, when my social studies class gave out comic awards, I received the "National Association for the Advancement of Cows and Pigs Award," mimicking the name of the famous civil rights organization. I was mildly embarrassed. It was the first time that the principal thing for which I had become known was my work concerning the socially-constructed, political notion of race and I wasn't sure how I felt about that. Besides, I wasn't sure that there wasn't some inherent racism in the naming of the award. Glenn Perkins had baptized me somehow in those few hours in his living room into a fellowship of consciousness that I had not imagined or sought, but from which I could not now release myself, and which would, in fact, affect me the rest of my life.

---

[i] Invitation to Sociology: A Humanistic Perspective by Peter Berger (Anchor Books, 1963)

1966

By 1965, I had left home, and wound up eventually living in a trailer park on the outskirts of Ft. Knox, Kentucky, married to a cook in the Army. The Viet Nam war had sucked tens of thousands of young men into military service, and there were lots of African-Americans on and around the base. When my husband's Sergeant, Bill Duncan, who happened to be one of them, found out that we were struggling pretty grimly on Specialist, 4th Class pay (two steps above a Private), he showed up unexpectedly one day with a carload of food. We were greatly moved and very grateful, and invited him and his wife over for dinner.

Our trailer, which was by no stretch of the imagination a "mobile home," was so small that you couldn't get to the bathroom if the refrigerator door was open. The bedroom was the size of the bed, the bathroom was the size of a pair of adult feet, and when the table was in place, whoever was sitting on the couch was trapped until it was moved. Nevertheless, the Duncans came for dinner and returned for card games and beer, and, eventually, to teach us the "Boomerang" while they regaled us with tales of Baltimore and how we really must come to see them when all of this was over. We promised to do so, of course, but we never did. We didn't last long enough as a couple. But the camaraderie we enjoyed on those many occasions in that tiny little trailer rivaled any that I have ever experienced anywhere else.

Life was difficult as an Army wife in the Viet Nam war era. The sum total of our entertainment budget was a subscription to Playboy magazine, with its high-end budget able to provide hundreds of pages of articles and short stories that took a long time to read. Drills to stay in continual readiness to leave for the Far East without any notice at all kept us holding our breath until the day we were released at the end of my husband's tour of duty as a draftee. The dinners and card games we shared with Bill and Bertha Duncan provided the only moments of relief in an otherwise stress-filled and poverty-stricken existence.

Everyone in the trailer park was related to the Army in some way, an Army where Black and White men and women were only too aware that they might wind up dying in each other's arms in a jungle someday. But it didn't stop the rumblings. I don't remember how the information was communicated, but I remember being eventually given to understand somehow that if we kept having those Negroes over, there was going to be trouble. The Duncans were two of the sweetest, best-hearted people I had ever met and I could not bear the thought of their being hurt in any way, even their feelings. I started taking roles at the Ft. Knox Little Theater and soon was gone even more than my husband.

Still, when we were home, warnings notwithstanding, we had the Duncans over anyway, and I recall sweatily dancing the "Boomerang" to Jr. Walker and the All-Stars till we dropped exhausted the night we said good-bye. We heard that the company shipped out shortly after we left town and I guess Bill Duncan went with them. I hope he lived and wound up back in Baltimore with Bertha where he belonged. But, even with the war making battlefield buddies out of all kinds of people, and even with the civil rights struggle forcing the pretense of progress on a nation that purported to accept it, I can't think today of the Duncans without remembering the warnings. My husband and I were being threatened because we were laughing and eating and dancing with people of color. Fifty years later, Black people and White people laughing and eating and dancing together still make many people crazy. But if it's so awful, why does **anyone** want to do it? If it's so inappropriate and outrageous, why would it occur to **any** of us to cross the line?

1968

After my husband and I split up and I started dating again, I was approached by a friend who was a student at a university near where I was living in West Palm Beach, Florida. Another student, someone I had never met, a medical student, actually, wanted a blind date for a party. I agreed to be his date. After all, here was a *med* student, someone operating in circles that seemed very magical to me at the time, circles that a young, working class woman longed to belong to, as well.

My friend explained that the young man in question was Black, but in 1968, many a White girl "crossed the line," as the practice was called, because to hold back would be to appear racist. And besides, hadn't I danced with Black guys at lunch ten years before and with Bill Duncan in a sweaty trailer in Kentucky? It felt like a big "so what?" to me.

He was an attractive enough guy and carried himself like the aspiring upper echelon professional that he was preparing to be. I imagine that he was used to getting his way with young women and he certainly got his way with me, after the party. I was hardly a virgin, after all, having already been married and divorced. And it wasn't as if I'd picked him up in a bar. But the morning "after," as I prepared myself to leave his apartment and return to my own, our conversation developed in ways that I did not expect.

Women in my generation were raised to believe that a woman is supposed to be married to some man — any man — rather than to be alone. Further, we were raised to believe that a woman must imagine that there is some possibility that a man is considering this before she gives him sexual favors. The possibility could be extremely thin and her imagination could be little more than a fantasy, denial on her part even, but she had to be able to pretend...or she was a whore. Needless to say, over the years, I have distanced myself greatly from this early teaching, but in my twenties, despite the sexual revolution within which I was a very good soldier, I lived, as most women did then, in a virtual la-la land of hopeful dreams for ultimate fulfillment as a wife.

So, after rubbing some toothpaste on my teeth in his bathroom, I broached the necessary subject of our "future." The young man quickly conveyed that there would be none. Puzzled, I asked him why he took me to bed if he had no intention of seeing me again. I know much more about these matters now than I did at the time, but still his answer shocked me — though, of course, I never let on. I don't remember his precise words, but they had something to do with the fact that I was White.

The thought stopped me cold. *He had bedded me because I was White?* I felt as if I was nothing more than a piece of meat. As an intelligent, liberal-leaning White woman, I recognized that African-Americans had been dealt a bad hand in the United States and were still being wrongly relegated to a position of inferiority at that time. It had never occurred to me, however, that an African-American might be angry about this, might feel some sort of disdain for one of *us* because of it or might want to place one of **us** in a reduced position.

I had no context into which to put this new experiential knowledge. So I went home, making a mental note to keep my distance from African-American men in the future until I could tell whether they were into me or just into my skin. I had no idea at the time the complexity of this issue or what the particulars of the complexity were, but eventually I did come to understand it better, though with great respect, like one has when one approaches fire or the ocean or a hurricane.

1973

I had spent an errant summer in Iowa City, Iowa, right after joining the masses of young people on the move in the United States in the late sixties and early seventies. Then, in only a matter of months, it was on to Boston, out to San Francisco, back across the country once more to Vermont, and ultimately back to Iowa City to recuperate from a car accident that occurred in a Vermont snow storm. As it happened, a national movement to reform and even abolish prisons had one of its principal hubs in Iowa City at this time, and as I was wont to do, I rapidly found and inculcated myself in a collective of intelligent and ferociously committed men and women at 505 South Lucas.

The National Prison Center had great impact with its Prisoners Digest International, its legal suits, and its connection to the Church of the New Song, an organization that was birthed in prison with the intent of creating a forum for prisoners to have positive effects on their own lives. As ordained ministers in the Church, protected by the First Amendment to the U.S. Constitution, and having many hundreds of members in state and federal prisons from coast to coast, we gained entry by court order into prison after prison: to speak, to negotiate, to counsel, to organize, and to encourage. The effort consumed us, eventually literally, taking every bit of energy and resources and, for some, sanity that we could muster through any means.

But one of many things that I learned going into the prisons was that the numbers of African-Americans compared to others was absolutely shocking. One had either to believe that African-Americans were unprincipled rapscallions widely incapable of socially acceptable behavior or one had eventually to believe that the criminal justice system across the board in every state in the union was shot through with institutionalized oppression against people of color in general and African-Americans most particularly. Convinced that the former was completely illogical, the latter took the education Glenn Perkins had given me ten years before and expanded it into terrifying proportions. It was horrifying. Was there no law? What in the world was being done to the African-American community? And why? I reeled under this new knowledge with no idea whatsoever of what to do with it or what its implications were.

Some years later, when I attended a Black Family Conference in Illinois because I was pregnant with my bi-racial daughter, I stood up in a large symposium on naming and addressing problems in the African-American community. I raised the issue of the criminal justice system and asked what the community was planning to do to address the miscarriage of justice that was putting so many men of color behind bars. One would have thought I had stood up and spoken in gibberish. My question and I were ignored. They simply were not yet prepared to discuss it as a group in public at that time, or at least not in response to someone that looked like me.

It was many years after that before I fully understood what a well-intended, but stupid thing I had done. African-Americans cannot *yet* count on the U.S. legal system to deal with them as fairly as with others. Police harassment and brutality in a range of forms remain common in African-American communities while little is done to mitigate the dire social state of those communities. It is a matter of repeated statistical record from coast to coast that African-Americans are more likely to be arrested, tried, convicted, and incarcerated for things that would not produce the same results for White people. In the face of such facts, what *can* African-Americans do? This is the law of the land we're talking about. If you can't trust the law of the land, what *can* you trust?

Going daily — by court order — into the maximum security penitentiary for men in Ft. Madison, Iowa, where more than half of the population came to the Sunday services we held, introduced me to a vast array of cultural and group norms and practices. I learned to discuss and understand legal cases like a lawyer. I learned to converse in "street," widely used among those in "the life," and varying in only minor ways from state to state. I learned to butt out of what was not my business. And I learned to sit in a room full of African-Americans as one person in a room full of people.

Sometimes people on the "outside" would ask, "Aren't you afraid in there?" And I always assured them that I was far safer in there than any of us are outside. Then I explained that the work we were doing was so appreciated by the prisoners that even the most mentally unbalanced among them would know better than to hurt one of us or make us want to go away. There was a covenant between us and the prisoners, at least half of whom were Black. We told them that, with the way the laws were being applied, any of us could be locked up. You're doing time for us, we would say. And we're at large for you.

Then, one day, walking down the aisle in an auditorium filled with more than four hundred prisoners sitting in respectful, but eager anticipation of the service we had prepared, I heard a voice float out over the crowd behind me. "You sure got big legs for a White girl..." The laughter that followed the comment, including my own, gave voice to the affection and trust that we had come to feel for each other.

Now the question is this: if the ritualized norm of institutionalized White Supremacy is "natural," then why do I — and the millions of others just like me — exist?

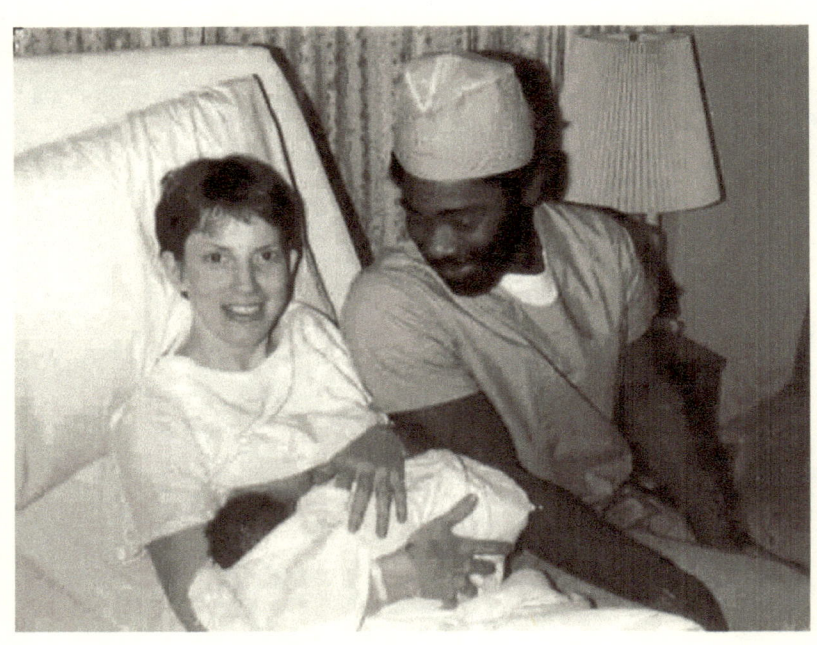

PART TWO

1981

In 1979, my two-year-old son, his father, and I moved from Rock Island, Illinois, to West Palm Beach, Florida. Within a matter of months, my son's father had descended into alcoholism even deeper than he had been before. When he pawned my electric typewriter while I was at work one day, I knew that I had to leave him. It was a messy parting. We had been together for five years and we had Eli, but I knew that, if I did not leave him, Eli would wind up with no sane parent at all.

So, without preparation, I found myself suddenly alone with a two-year-old boy to raise on $4 per hour. We slept together in a single bed in an apartment with the toilet in the kitchen and no stove at all. I drank hot water instead of coffee in the morning at my desk at work and had one piece of toast for breakfast. I was an emotional wreck. Eli's father had threatened to kill me in front of our son on our last night together. And Christmas had been utterly destroyed by his drinking. I desperately needed tenderness, not to mention help, and, when I met and started to date a charming and very handsome man named John, I gave no thought at all to his being Black.

Then, my parents came for a visit and John took us all out to dinner. Walking into the restaurant with John carrying my White son, I wondered what my parents were going to say to him, or to me later.

My mother, as it turned out, was extremely uncomfortable with John's race. My father's question to her was didn't she think that I was old enough (at 33 years of age) to decide who I wanted to be with. Shortly afterward, I discovered that John was married and I stopped seeing him, but my mother wasn't off the hook because a year later, I returned to Rock Island, began to date, and got pregnant by another African-American man. It turned her world upside down.

I had originally hired Ray, who eventually became my daughter's father, to work under me at a Community Action Agency where I had been a last minute choice to run a federal program. He was soft-spoken, intelligent, and looked like Teddy Pendergrass, complete with full beard. I was almost immediately smitten, but I was determined not to get involved with him because of our professional relationship at work. We managed to get through the first couple of months successfully, but when I finally invited him to my apartment for some reason or other, we rapidly became deeply involved, first emotionally and then sexually.

When I became pregnant in a matter of weeks, we were both thrilled. Ray bought me a gauzy purple and gold shirt from India to celebrate and I worked blissfully throughout the pregnancy, relishing the idea that this wonderful new life to whom I was about to give birth would be a bi-racial child. I was so in love with Ray that I would have been blissful in any case, but this Black child that I carried embodied my challenge to the society in which we lived, a society that demanded and *yet* demands on many levels and in both racial camps that Black people and White people remain socially segregated.

As the months passed, we experienced the struggles that bi-racial couples always face. We would sit down in a restaurant, for example, only to wait and wait and wait because no one would come to the table to take our order. Ray would become furiously indignant and I, new to this level of self-consciousness, would try to soothe and quiet him. That he had a right to his indignation never occurred to me at the time. That his frustration and irritation were, moreover, *appropriate* only finally occurs to me now.

But the most difficult issues, in any case, were the ones we carried within us, the tensions between us in spite of our love. Ray admitted to me that he didn't like White people, that he really had no idea how he had wound up with me, and that he had told his sister only a matter of months before meeting me that he knew one thing for certain: **he** would never get a White woman pregnant. He laughed about it, but it was apparent that it bothered him. And I became increasingly aware that he was always feeling my Whiteness, whether we were alone or in public.

When we would be walking together downtown where we worked, his face and body language would manifest his embarrassment at being an African-American man seen by other African-Americans as having abandoned his people to mate with one of the "enemy." We didn't discuss this much. We didn't have to. Besides, I couldn't possibly have understood, and I suspect that, just as he said, he honestly could not compute our relationship in the face of his fierce desire not to have found himself in it. But, in any case, he was educating me still further in Black culture, without meaning to, without effort on either of our parts.

I would notice him giving a small, jerky nod of solidarity to other African-Americans and I would feel the strength of that solidarity. I was proud to be with him, even if he was not proud to have me there. I was beginning to perceive African-American people as having miraculously and valiantly survived a long and arduous journey through a wilderness I would never know. I felt honored to have been chosen to walk beside one of these brave survivors, whatever the stress we carried. And I felt doubly honored to have been chosen by history to carry a Black child into being.

We had long intellectual conversations about all manner of topics and occasionally were able to make forays into the topic of race, as well. Once, when we were talking about police presence in the inner city, he asked me, "Do you know what 'garrison forces' are?"

"No," I admitted.

"Garrisons are military forces that are sent in during an occupation to keep order over a conquered people," he explained. "That's the way a lot of *us* see the police." I felt like a child peeping through a doorway crack at a room she is not allowed to enter. I soaked up his input like a sponge. But it was to be short lived.

One blow that undermined our relationship occurred on the job. My boss, the Executive Director of the Community Action Agency where Ray and I worked, called me in when my pregnancy became apparent and told me that if I didn't fire my baby's father, he would. He claimed that my other twelve employees would not respect me as long as they knew that Ray and I were personally involved outside of work.

Had I known then what I know now about life, I would have told him simply that he was wrong. My staff was completely supportive of Ray and me, and worked harder than any other program team in the agency. Further, they had all demonstrated their respect for Ray by voting unanimously to give him the only promotion that had become available during the program year. Had my boss stood firm in the face of my arguments, I know now that I should have forced *him* to fire Ray, or even threatened to quit myself. But I was so taken off guard that I did neither. I somehow imagined that the blow of losing his job would be gentler coming from me. What a terrible mistake!

In retrospect, I realize that I emasculated Ray by firing him, something that would not be easy for him to come to grips with while I was going to work every day and he was receiving unemployment benefits. That I had done it myself, rather than require that my boss do it, put a treacherous male/female spin on the ball. Worse, I could not possibly remove the "race card" from the situation, no matter how oblivious I was to its presence. Regardless of how I saw it, Ray's firing could certainly be seen as the punishment he was dealt for having impregnated his White boss, who was not being similarly punished.

While all of this was going on, my parents had been in Florida for the winter. When they arrived back in Illinois in late spring to find their oldest daughter pregnant by an African-American man to whom she was not married, my mother became frantic. She wept. She mentioned a Black couple at her church that was looking to adopt a child. She told me that she was mortified, that she couldn't face her friends, that she and my father were putting their house up for sale. She refused to meet Ray. She would not allow him to accompany me to their house for dinner. She refused to come to the apartment we were now sharing, and indeed, would sit in the car when she came to get Eli for a visit, rather than risk coming up the stairs and having Ray answer the door. She even refused to meet us in a restaurant on "neutral ground." This was not helping matters for Ray and me in our attempts to create and cement our relationship.

My response was unavoidable. I stopped going to my parents' house. I suggested that my mother get new friends. And finally, I told her sadly that I was sorry that she felt the way she did, but that I wasn't doing this to hurt her and that I was happy about the baby, which was not a litter of pups to give away, after all, but my child.

When my sister wrote a letter asking whether or not she would be able to maintain her very special relationship with Eli after the new baby came, I wrote a response to the entire family. I outlined in no uncertain terms that it was more important to me that my children bond to each other than that they bond with the extended family and that, if I got any sense whatsoever that they were treating the new baby differently from Eli, I would withdraw both children from family activities. When I picked up Eli at my parents' house after giving birth to his little sister, my mother handed me a blanket that she had crocheted for her new grandchild and I hoped that this act heralded a resolution of our stand-off. It did not.

In retrospect, I realize that there was no way that Ray could or would or even should have tried to assimilate into a family situation so fraught with negativism toward him. But after our daughter, Morgan Rae, was born, I boldly asked him to marry me anyway and he moved out. I was devastated. I went on welfare because I wanted to nurse and be with her the way I had been with Eli in his early years. I was so poor that I was forced to do the laundry — including Eli's school clothes — in the bathtub and hang it out on the porch railings. Ray had a diaper service delivered until Morgan outgrew diapers, which was an immense assistance, but other than that, plus Christmas and birthday gifts, and occasional babysitting, he was in no position financially to do much more.

By now I was living in a poor and racially-mixed neighborhood, which was all I could afford, and I badly needed my parents' help, however begrudging, but after nearly two years of trying to get my mother to accept Ray, I finally just withdrew entirely from her. And shortly after that, I actually prayed about the situation, something I don't often do. The answer I received was that the problem was not between her and me, but between her and God. I imagined her getting on her knees, railing against God for allowing me to get pregnant by a Black man. I smiled and shook my head. "Poor Mom," I thought. "She's insulting the One who created all life in the Universe — including Black people."

She would call to say hello, offering to take me shopping or whatever. I would reply simply that we were fine and didn't need anything — far, far from true. She would sign off by saying that she loved me. I assured her that I loved her, as well, and we would hang up. And these occasional non-conversations were the sum total of our contact for several months.

Then, one day, there was a knock at my door. It was my mother, carrying a loaf of bread and a green plant. She apologized and begged for my forgiveness. She had been having trouble sleeping, she said. Then she went on to say that God had told her she was wrong, and to prove to me that she was sorry, she was offering me the use of her car for a month. She told me that she would have given it to me outright, but that my father had said no.

She went on to explain that she really wasn't racist anyway, that she grew up playing with Black children who squatted on her father's land in Kentucky. They liked her so much, she said, that they had called her "Miss Ann." I almost laughed. I didn't tell her that "Miss Ann" is a pejorative term African-Americans often use to describe the quintessentially racist, though often clueless, White woman. Anyway, the children probably called her "Miss Ann" because the Black Codes of the south required that African-Americans call *all* White people Miss and Mister, even the children. But I didn't want to spoil her moment. It was enough.

When my mother finally invited Ray over for dinner, he turned down the invitation, and in fact, I'm not sure I remember him ever going to my parents' house, but ultimately, my mother and father did eventually come to celebrations at my home when Ray was present and we all ate and told jokes and played cards together. Still, it was too late for Ray and me. When he finally proposed to me, I said no immediately. I didn't even give him the respect of my consideration. I have always suspected that I said 'no' largely because of a situation that developed a year after Morgan's birth.

It was Christmas day. There was three feet of new snow on the ground and the temperature was below zero. Ray had spent several hours, bundled to the teeth and freezing, riding city buses and standing at bus stops in the bitter wind, carrying multiple bags of brightly wrapped Christmas gifts. I had not expected him, and the surprise of seeing him there when I answered the door in that terrible weather was part of his present to all of us.

Even if the weather had not made it difficult for him to leave, the Christmas excitement, after the children had gone to bed, propelled us into my bedroom, and six weeks later, I learned at a clinic that I was, indeed, pregnant by Ray again. I was overwhelmed and distraught. I called him at my apartment where he was watching Eli and Morgan while I saw the doctor. Weeping over the phone, I agonized rhetorically, "How could this *happen*?"

What I meant, of course, was that I had just begun to feel that maybe my ducks were finally getting in a row, after all. I now had a decent place to live and enough money to live on, the children were becoming more independent, and I was beginning to think about my future. I took Ray's answer as a flip remark at the time, but I think he was probably referring to much, much more truth than I was willing to consider. "You know exactly how this happened," he said.

Our subsequent conversation at his apartment was more painful. I asked him point blank if he loved me. "Not the way you mean," he replied.

"Then I have to get an abortion," I responded calmly. "I can't raise three children by myself — I'm struggling now. You'll have to give me half of what it costs."

Ray gave me the two hundred dollars that represented his half of the fee for the procedure and I had the abortion. I knew that I did not have the financial, emotional, or psychological resources to take on the responsibility of another baby at that time, especially with Morgan hardly more than a year old herself, but I felt the loss deeply. And though I was not angry with Ray afterward for not "loving" me in the way that I "meant," I believed that, had he been willing to commit that February morning when the question was asked, we would have survived — all of us, including the new baby — and our lives would have been quite different than they eventually turned out. I think that it was out of this belief — right or wrong — that I declined his offer of marriage.

I tried to maintain contact with Ray through the years, even though Morgan had not been able to see him since she was seven-years-old. We had moved to Florida that year so that I could continue graduate school, but we eventually lost each other about the time she left home for college.

One of his sisters told me at one point that he had taken to being a recluse of sorts, growing his hair long and writing a book in a bedroom at another sister's apartment. It made me sad because I regret whatever part I may have played in alienating this gentle, deep, and decent man. Our last conversations before we lost touch were amazingly reminiscent of those we had had back when we were first in each other's lives.

I could play "what if" forever with Ray's and my relationship. What if I had not participated in Ray's firing from his job at the Community Action Agency where we worked? What if my mother had not been so opposed to him because of his race? What if it hadn't taken Ray so long to overcome his discomfort with *my* race? But none of it mattered in the end. And this is just the sort of damage that often gets done when the "color line" is crossed in our society.

1979

1983

Moving back to Rock Island, into the neighborhood where my family had moved back in 1956, had a strange quality of homecoming for me. The 100-year-old elementary school I had attended had been torn down, of course, and replaced by a more contemporary model, but the ancient trees and the big, old houses, many of which had now been split into upstairs and downstairs duplexes, were still there, as were some of the bumpy brick streets. The bulk of the neighborhood did not appear to be as abjectly poverty-stricken as I was. And I was too determined to change the racist face of our society to let the fact that the neighborhood had a high percentage of African-American residents bother me. Eli only had to walk a couple of blocks to school. And I was soon playing a functional role in the community.

To begin with, I came across and joined a large Presbyterian church that demonstrated a profound commitment to the people that had over time moved in around it. This was very unusual for me, as I had walked away from organized religion when I left my parents' house at eighteen years of age. But I was moved by the real candles burning in the darkly wooded sanctuary and the minister's kind words about the church having a responsibility to meet the needs of all God's children by reaching out and not just waiting for them to come. In addition, I needed to belong somewhere and the church helped to provide that in the early days after my little family and I arrived.

I was also looking for ways to be useful. Even though I was now on welfare, I was used to working hard, and not always for pay. The years in the prison movement, for example, had required intense levels of work by every member of the collective, but nobody received a paycheck. We lived in the house, ate, bought cigarettes, even paid for drugs using money from some nameless pool of funding that belonged to none of us in particular. And all we were expected to offer in return was our every waking moment of attention to the task at hand. I had lived the same way for a short time at an underground newspaper collective in San Francisco before that. So I was well familiar with using my unencumbered time to accomplish something. And it didn't take me long to find several commitments besides the church.

I wrote for a range of alternative newspapers, for one thing, including the local Black weekly: feature articles, reviews — whatever got me out and about and involved — and even sometimes columns with a radical political tinge to them. This gave me an introduction into a number of circles, one of which was the Rock Island branch of the A. Phillip Randolph Institute, an African-American organization named after the labor leader who organized the March on Washington where Martin Luther King, Jr., gave his "I Have A Dream" speech.

The Institute worked in Rock Island to register and get out the Black vote, to facilitate relations between labor unions and Black workers, and at one point, to bring in the

United States Justice Department for a public forum to discuss police department policies and practices related to people of color.

"Progressive discipline to deal with individual incidents is not the answer," I was quoted on the front page of the Rock Island Argus the following morning. "The real problem is an attitude problem of police concerning Blacks. Residents need a police force to believe in. Racism cannot be tolerated. All officers must know that slavery is dead in America." It wasn't long before I was being approached to speak, to write, and to advise.

Eventually, I even created some campaign materials and speeches for a young African-American man who wanted to run for a position on the school board. We generated far more than the usual number of votes to put someone in that position, but, in the effort to prevent his election, the opposing party managed to bring out unprecedented numbers of voters at the very last minute to defeat him. We were impressed with ourselves and our efforts. He might not have won, but we had made the local establishment feel our breath.

When a former workmate of mine, an African-American woman named Esther, found out about my situation, she came to see me at my rat- and roach-infested apartment. I had painted it all — the walls and even the floor — and turned around the door lock so that it couldn't be removed with a screwdriver from the outside. But she was aghast at my poverty and took me in hand at once to teach me the ropes of the public assistance system.

I had lived there for approximately a year. Eli was being tormented by angry little Black boys who, even though smaller than him, had enough street-sense and rage to brutalize him on a regular basis. I explained to him where it was all coming from in terms of the past and present White

Supremacy against which they were reacting, but that doubtless did not make the grass he was sometimes forced to eat taste any better. Before we left the neighborhood, he had found his own unwillingness to suffer, and learned how to protect himself in ways that ultimately resulted a decade later in his becoming a member of a Black gang.

As an attractive, naïve, unattached, and poverty-stricken young woman with an African-American baby, new to the neighborhood, I was seen as "fair game" by lower class African-American men with even a little money and charm, and was taken advantage of accordingly. I was lost in the wilderness on the other side of what W.E.B. Dubois had called, in 1903, "the color-line." And up until Esther stepped in, I was left, much like Eli, to make my own way and take my embarrassing lumps with the territory, trying, most of the time unsuccessfully, to maintain whatever dignity I could, under the circumstances.

My situation notwithstanding, I managed to sell a campaign speech to the incumbent mayor of Rock Island, who was also my landlord, my son's school principal, and an African-American man himself. The speech was so beautiful, he said, that he was going to have to memorize rather than paraphrase it. But that did not change the fact that I was scrubbing my son's jeans in the bathtub in the apartment he was renting to me.

Being very, very poor is a difficult space in which to find oneself, no matter what one looks like. And certainly, many African-Americans make a good living. But the statistics tell us that African-American men are nearly four times more likely to be unemployed at every educational level. And many African-Americans were and are being educated in schools so lacking in their capacity to offer a truly adequate education that the students who pass through them are virtually guaranteed not to be able to compete with most White students, many of whom do not have those same obstacles.

Without realizing it, then, I was receiving an education of my own: what it feels like to have few options, to not be able to protect your children, to be the butt of jokes at the hands of your "betters," to have your intelligence appear as a surprise, to have to live in slum-lord housing, to have to act like you don't notice what is being done to you, to watch in wonder as police march in formation with dogs down your street at one o'clock in the morning — practicing, sending messages. In short, I was taking "Ghetto Life 101." And Esther had come to give me the follow-up course: "Navigating the System" or "Public Aid R Us"

"Good grief!" Esther said, shaking her head as she took me in hand. "You don't have to live like this!" And a few months later, she had me ensconced in privately-owned, federally-subsidized housing on the outskirts of a nearby community, in a brand new two story three-bedroom townhouse with a bath-and-a-half and a patio with a view, where they paid *me* a dollar a month to live there. I was so flabbergasted that I tip-toed around the place for the first three days as if I had sneaked my way in or something.

I had left our couch in Rock Island because it was full of mice, and we moved into our new home with only beds for the children, a dining table and chairs, a double bed mattress for me to sleep on, and a wooden rocking chair. Still, between my newly subsidized rent, my small public assistance check, and the food stamps I was getting (a whopping dollar per meal for each of us), we were now high-rolling. New washers and dryers stood in the laundry room across the street — and I could afford to use them! There were woods for Eli to play in with new friends, little ones for Morgan to get to know, and a fancy new Publix grocery store right across the highway to take the place of the ghetto supermarket I had grown used to.

One thing that I couldn't help but notice after my immediately previous experience, though, was that there were practically no African-Americans in the complex. I can only speculate as to why that was. It was, after all, on the outskirts of a small, largely White suburban community with no bus line. And there were many White factory workers who had recently been laid off, were in dire straits, and must certainly have rushed to apply for the slots when the complex opened. Still, I was sure there were lots of people of color who would have wanted to live there, as well, and who would have qualified for the complex. But where were they? Aside from my daughter and one family who lived on the other side of the circle, who knew? Then, I invited Jasper to move in.

I had met Jasper hanging out down in East Moline, a Black-er neighborhood than where I was now living. I had gone to East Moline in the first place because Rock Island was at least a thirty-minute drive from where I now lived and I really missed the nightlife — dancing to rhythm and blues music in clubs on Saturday nights. I had grown up dancing to rhythm and blues in school, but as an adult, I found that White clubs tended toward rock and roll, so I went looking and found the music and dancing I preferred.

By the time I had shown up at one of the clubs in East Moline several times, one of the local men looked across at me from the end of the bar and said, "So...you're one of the regulars now?" and I nodded yes. I was less emotionally and financially needy than I had been when I first arrived in the "hood" in Rock Island. I was somewhat less naïve, as well. But I was still a White girl in a Black world and had many miles to go before I would sleep.

Jasper called me over to him in the park where I was watching my children play late one afternoon. He had several men standing on either side and slightly behind him while he was seated at a picnic table under a rectangular umbrella-style roof. He carried himself for all the world like a man in a god-father movie. He was dead serious and I was a sucker for drama.

"Who's your man?" he intoned in a bored, but very direct voice, looking straight into my eyes.

I belligerently answered that I saw who I pleased.

He asked me again in the same tone of voice. "Who's your man?"

I assured him that I found a man unnecessary.

But the third time he asked, obviously not to be put off, I admitted simply, looking down, "I don't have one."

Jasper and I spoke a few times after that on the phone, which I could now afford to have, or sitting in his car in the shade behind a school in the early evening hours. But we didn't get involved until after my hysterectomy. When I came out of the anesthesia, sweaty and with my mouth full of fuzz, I found a card and a box of candy from Jasper sitting on the side table. Several days later, my mother brought me home from the hospital and before she could even leave, Jasper walked into my townhouse with a whole watermelon.

First of all, I was greatly embarrassed because I hardly knew him, he had never been in my home before, and he walked in like he was used to doing so — right in front of my mother, though she was reticent by this time to say anything about it. Secondly, I was confused about the melon. A *whole* watermelon? I thought. What am I going to do with a *whole* watermelon? Eli was staying with my mother and Morgan had gone with her father to spend a few weeks with his sister in Decatur while I was recuperating.

As it turned out, that watermelon was all I wanted to eat — day after day — until it was gone. I suspect now that this is an old country wives' treatment. Jasper's family was from

Georgia and he still lived with his mother, a wise and sensible matriarch, greatly respected by her children. The watermelon was cold and sweet and made me feel satisfied, but digested and was passed easily, something that was, as it turned out, of crucial importance after my surgery. Jasper and I read and played cards and watched television and talked for hours until I healed, by which time, he had simply moved in.

Jasper had spent seven years in prison for manslaughter when a man died after they had a fight, but I was not intimidated by the thought of a man's having been to prison. Through my work with the National Prison Center and the Church of the New Song, I had met and come to know literally hundreds of men, particularly Black men, who had had that experience. He only had a part-time job washing dishes at a restaurant, but with his income and my public assistance, we created a home.

When I threw a Christmas party that year with a seven-foot real evergreen tree decorated with white origami cranes (representing peace) so that each of the thirty or forty guests could take one home as a party favor, Jasper was a huge hit. He was an excellent host that night and when I think of him, I always remember the way he fit in with all those largely educated people I knew from other circles in my life. He moved from conversation to conversation, making sure everybody had what they needed, including me, before finally sitting down to play chess with a writer I knew.

It was that Jasper that made me withdraw from him. He deserved better than a woman who was just going to be there for a while. I cared a lot for him and fantasized sometimes what our wedding would look like. But despite his ability to move among the range of party-goers at Christmas, in my heart of hearts, I knew by this time that I was headed for a much different life at some point and that we would not go there together. I did not realize yet that I would shortly be in college, that I would complete a bachelor's degree in a calendar year, and that I would leave this community for graduate school, but I knew in my gut that I was headed somewhere and that I would go alone. I told him so and he moved out, but he didn't believe it.

Several months later, I went down to a bar where we were both well known, had one too many drinks, picked up the owner's son (who was visiting from Washington, D.C., and who was tending bar that night) and took him back to my place to have sex. A few days later, Jasper called. He wanted to pick up his chess set, he said. He walked in, talked with me for fifteen or twenty minutes and then proceeded to beat me up in my own front yard.

He kept asking me why I had done this thing, this having sex with somebody that knew him, that he knew, so that all of our mutual acquaintances were aware of it. In a most cavalier fashion, I had put Jasper in a position where he felt he had to humiliate me in public as I had humiliated and wounded him. A man fully capable of killing me with a blow, he withheld the true force of his outrage, only splitting my lip and loosening my teeth and scaring me and my poor children out of our wits while my neighbors stood around and watched.

I called the police, who took one look at my pale skin and one look at his mug shot and told me that he would be out of jail before I got out of the emergency room. I asked if they were going to take a photograph of my face and they declined, explaining that the judge wasn't going to do anything anyway.

"You might as well get a gun," they told me, "if you really want to protect yourself. There's only so much we can do and we can't be around here all the time."

I was amazed at their nonchalance and I was terrified of what Jasper might do in the future, not understanding that he had already done all that he needed to do. Even the District Attorney's office told me that the judge would take no action when I went to court. They didn't even send a prosecutor to the hearing, so someone who knew absolutely nothing about the case had to stand up as a placeholder in order for the proceedings to occur.

To everyone's collective amazement, the judge listened to me, dressed Jasper down in court, demanded that he pay my $700 emergency room bill, sent him to spend the week-end in jail (in deference to his job), and warned him that if he touched or bothered me again, he would return to prison. When I recounted all of this to a representative of the District Attorney's office, they were incredulous. Jasper wound up going to Atlanta for a year to avoid the potential for subsequent problems, though he found me once after he returned and apologized.

"I was so hurt," he said. "You do understand that, don't you? You hurt me so badly, I wanted to hurt you back. I couldn't help it. I wanted *you* to feel what *I* felt."

But I was unable to do more than to just forgive him. The trauma of the experience was too great for me to overcome immediately.

I know much now what I didn't know then, as do we all. We are learning as a society that anything that would be illegal between two men in a bar downtown must be illegal between a man and a woman in a living room — or a front yard — even if they have loved each other. I am sure that if the incident had occurred last month instead of thirty years ago, it would have been handled by the police and the prosecutors quite differently.

But the fact is, nonetheless, that one of the reasons they treated me the way they did — and this was made absolutely clear to me at the time — was that I was White and Jasper was Black. I have learned that, even now, when a White woman mates with a Black man, on a very basic level she is seen as forfeiting her right to protection from him or from any other African-American. "That's what she gets," the society seems to say. It was my appropriate punishment for crossing the line. That would teach me.

There's an old saying about women who go with African-American men. It's supposed to be crude and sexual and declares knowingly with a sly wink that "once you go *Black*, you'll never go *back*." Well, not if you're being punished for going Black in the first place, you won't.

1984

Somehow, in the middle of all this madness, a presence burst into my consciousness in the person of Calvin Hernton. Calvin was a truly brilliant man, an African-American sociologist who had already become an established part of the New York City poetry scene while I was still doing a term paper on racial discrimination at my virtually entirely White Midwestern high school in the 1960's. But I came across him first while doing research on interracial relationships for a book I thought I was going to write on the subject nearly twenty years later.

I had been invited to speak somewhere on my research and was quite methodically gathering information from a number of sources when I discovered <u>Sex and Racism in America</u>, Calvin's much touted electric polemic first published in 1963 and still in print in multiple languages. Two paragraphs into it, I looked over at Ray, sitting on the other side of the kitchen and, said "Listen to this...," proceeding to read the introduction aloud. Seven hours later, after passing the book back and forth between us, we finished reading the whole thing at one sitting, out loud, and we were so mind-blown that we couldn't even discuss it.

I wrote the author immediately, gushing about how amazing his work was and how it had affected me. I went on to describe the book that I was trying to write and mailed the letter without much expectation that it would necessarily be answered. Perusing the card catalogue at the library for other Hernton books, I soon had another in hand, Coming Together: Black Power, White Hatred, and Sexual Hang-ups, that he had published in 1971, an answer of sorts to the glut of letters he had received in response to his earlier work. In it, he unapologetically mentioned that he simply didn't respond to his readers who wrote him, that he couldn't really because of the sheer numbers involved, but that he didn't care to, in any case, and I shrugged. I hadn't expected to distinguish myself from the pack and had never written an author before anyway, though I had read many, many books.

A couple of months went by and, much to my astonishment, I received in the mail from Calvin Hernton six 8" X 14" pages of lined notebook paper covered with single-spaced typing. I read it standing next to the mailbox on the concrete steps outside my apartment in the ghetto, tingling with excitement that this behemoth of intelligence had deigned to write his humble, well, if not servant, at least awe-struck follower, signing the letter, "Sincerely yours, Calvin." I was breathless.

Eventually, many years later, I learned by reading the prologue for something he was writing for publication that he had been coming back to life at that time after burying himself emotionally over the death of his ex-wife, who he felt he had ill served. But I couldn't know that at the time. Nor would he have told me. We had another dance to do.

Letters and phone calls flashed back and forth between us. Accompanying his letters, he would return copies of my own letters back to me with notes all over them as if they were papers that he had graded for one of his students at Oberlin College, where he was a popular professor and writer-in-residence writing letters to a woman on welfare. In one of his early missives, he wrote,

> *"One thing though, and I say this with humility, you can <u>write</u>; I am impressed; yet a whole lot of people would-be-writers but never actually write, or if so, they never follow through — they get discouraged, and cease and grow silent. Unless you are very lucky, being a writer takes, in addition to ability, talent, sensitivity, etc., a lot of long suffering tenacity. In other words, you got to be crazy, absolutely nuts."*

A later outburst, my favorite of those I received between 1983 and 2001 said,

> *"Hi. Hello. Goddamnit why you write such fantastic letter! Why you you! Frankly I don't know about you, buddy...he, he, he. JessssUs, lawdamercy, your words jump right off the page and get all inside of my clothes, sentences, images, feelings, emotions, mentations, guts, blood flow, jump right off the page and get inside all over my body throughout.*

> *"What's this/ 'The glorious cerebrality of it all tooth on jowl with the banality of the mechanics.' What's that? Eh? You better watch shit like that — I'm liable to steel it! Like this:*

> *Photo of Your Last Letter*
> *(a prooem, stolen from B, given back to her)*
> *   Glorious cerebrality*

Tooth on jowl
The banality of the mechanics
Joys and horrors
The blessing/curse of snobbery
Born of feeling different —
The writer watches..."

The first time of seven or eight that we actually saw each other face to face, he interrupted me in the middle of a sentence at one point to blurt sternly, "Look here! You can sell yourself short all you want to. I can't do anything about that. But *I* ain't gonna pretend you've got no brain!" I came back from Oberlin changed for all time and ultimately entered college at the age of thirty-eight as a direct result of the effect those words had on me.

Once I began, I earned 106 credit hours via a non-traditional degree program at Western Illinois University which, added to the 14 credits I had chalked up twenty years before, allowed me to graduate with a Bachelor's degree in twelve months. Nobody was more surprised than me. And I shortly found myself having breakfast with Calvin in Detroit, talking about what I should concentrate on in graduate school while I studied sociology, a career trajectory I had chosen largely because that's what he had studied. Still, he warned me that he wasn't sure I would ever get anything much written. "A writer has to spend a lot of time alone," he told me. "And I'm not sure you could stand the isolation."

Over the years, besides Detroit, we spent long week-ends in Chicago and New York City and visited each other's homes. And we spent hour after hour on telephones late into the night when Calvin and I were most likely to be awake anyway. Eventually, he invited me to spend a summer living somewhere together, in the thought that we'd see what it was like and whether or not our relationship could become more than it was, but I declined. Calvin always seemed to be loving more than one woman at a time and, while I absolutely believed that he loved us all, I wasn't sure that I could deal with this over the long haul and told him so. "Well, you're not wrong to be concerned," was his reply.

More to the point, actually, though, was the fact that I was simply incapable of being in a real relationship myself. Calvin and I were two wounded birds in many ways, flying in the same sky, with no land in sight and wearying wings. Over a Chinese dinner one evening, I told him that he was like an island in my mind where I could take a vacation whenever I wanted and, shortly afterward, he sent me a new edition of his first book with the sentiment repeated on the flyleaf. But when he called me on the spur of the moment once to meet him for even one day anywhere, I told him no, weeping over my own frustration with wanting to be able to give him more than I seemed to be able to give.

The last time I saw Calvin was in Tallahassee in 1993, when I brought him to Florida State University as a featured lecturer for a series on cutting edge issues related to race. I put him up at a motel near where I was living at the time with another man. We all had dinner together and Calvin and I had little time alone, but when I took him to the airport, he turned in the doorway before boarding and kissed me full on the mouth without warning. He did not hesitate, but I would not have denied him, and now I am immensely grateful that he gave me that momentary blessing and farewell.

Eight years later, again without warning to me, Calvin died of cancer. Knowing that I had spoken with him while he lay dying and he did not tell me underscored the terrible distances between us, and once again defined the man that he always was. He told me that he had finally married a woman he had loved for a long time and I was glad for him. Then, in 2000, he sent me a note expressing his sadness over

Eli's death with a copy of his last book of poems, but he still did not say that he was dying, too. I simply came across on the internet one day an announcement of an event to memorialize Calvin Hernton's life. I took the day off work and spent it with our memories.

So, how does my remembrance of him relate to the book I am finally, finally writing? Perhaps it is primarily the matter that it took an African-American intellect to awaken my own. Calvin called the similarities between racism and sexism "the scarlet analogy" and often spoke and wrote as a womanist and anti-sexist, long before I had a clear idea of what either was. But he also named the demons that dance around the socially-constructed political notion of race — one by one — in ways that maybe no one else ever will. And he did it, first and foremost, by writing the truth and, most particularly and with great self-consciousness, the truth about himself. To attempt to do the same thing myself all these decades later, to write this book, full of stories about Ray and Jasper and Morgan and the others, when the garden of my mind was cultivated by the likes of Calvin Hernton, without giving him his due as a man of magnitude and honoring him for making this effort possible would be unconscionable.

On the other hand, he was most absolutely just a man, and a southern-born African-American man at that. To look into his eyes when you could catch him without his dark glasses was to know that he had suffered, but he shared it little with me. I was so impossibly self-centered and White, and he was so private and kind, that I will never know what it would have been to truly know him. It was my loss and, like losing Eli, one I will carry until I, too, die.

But a far greater loss, perhaps, is the one that represents what the world could have celebrated in Calvin Hernton had he not been so tormented because of his race. What might he have written had he not gotten up every morning of his life to the Medusa head of racial oppression? What planets would he have soared beyond with that poet's mind of his had he not had to tote that barge and lift that bale in his heart of hearts?

The bottom line for me is that when I sat on his hallway floor in semi-darkness while he slept, reading "The Coming of Chronos to the House of Nightsong," the epic poem he wrote in 1964 about a southern White woman turning 100 while she thinks about her Black once-lover, the father of her child, I knew that he had seen, long before he knew me or I knew myself, into the soul of womanhood.

> *"The double dying of she who rides*
> *in the middle of the wind*
> *will reign in the world like an idiot fire*
> *And every woman sees in whichever*
> *man she gives her sex*
> *the potentiality of her whorehood."*

Because of that, if nothing else, I want to live up to the potential he saw in me. His loneliness, his torment, his willingness to examine and be examined, and his patience demands it.

1985

Just before I started going to college, I met, married, and divorced in rapid succession a real dyed-in-the-wool con artist. His name was Darryl. He was a light-skinned African-American man, 6'6" tall, who presented himself as a former Black Panther with a Master's degree in psychology from an African university. We talked politics and race and I was convinced that here, at last, was my soulmate: a radical mind who had been tried in the fire of prison, as so many African-American radical intellectual men have been, but who was fully capable of moving into the future unbroken and unbowed.

When he was arrested for a technical violation of his parole, I stood across the street from the jail with my children to encourage him on the other side of the bars, our fists in the air for him — and all the world — to see. Then, when he was moved briefly to the penitentiary at Joliet before he effected his own release again — much to the astonishment of his parole officer — I visited him and wrote him magical letters filled with political and sexual innuendo. And as soon as he was released, we married.

Within a matter of weeks after the wedding, he had me backed to the wall in our bedroom screaming insults at me for hours until the manager of the complex reported to me that my neighbors had begun to ask if I was "all right." Esther was afraid for my life. And after I read a book outlining how men with his type of childhood family relations grow up to brutalize women in very specific and chartable ways, I realized that she was right to be afraid. But by the time I read the book, he had already admitted to me that he had lied about his age, about his crimes, about his degree, and about his political history. He had completely fooled me *and* a team of psychological professionals at a mental health clinic where we had sought "couples counseling," as well!

I will never know for certain what possessed him to finally admit the truth to me rather than carrying out the charade even further. He was, he said, so ashamed of what he had done to me that he moved out, offering me one hundred dollars per month for one year and assuring me that he would draw up the divorce papers himself for me to file, if I would agree to wait until he went to court on the parole matter the following spring.

In retrospect, I think he was probably trying to make sure that I did not complicate his legal situation in negative ways and I suspect, as well, that he was trying to protect his position on the campaign team of an incumbent Congressman. In any case, I didn't tell anyone his secrets. We got divorced, as he said we would, and I moved on with my life.

What I learned from him was that any human can be mentally unbalanced, but that institutionalized oppression in the name of racism creates monsters all its own, and that the combination of the two is frightening indeed, not to be understated, and nothing to play with. In an article entitled "Dynamite Growing Out of Their Skulls,"[i] Calvin Hernton wrote in the 1960s that, if U.S. society didn't stop the racist oppression of African-Americans, an entire generation of Black youth would eventually manifest what he called "the psychology of the damned." He warned that they would be unreasonable, unwilling or unable to negotiate, and dangerous because they would, he predicted, see themselves as having nothing left to lose.

Even after I read his lines, I did not at that time realize the connections between his foreboding analysis and my experiences with Jasper and Darryl. I do now. Though we may see much more graphically in the present what Calvin was referring to, Jasper and Darryl were already tainted with the mark of the beast, as it were. There was no way either story could have ended any differently.

It was approximately this same time and just before I decided to start going to school that I overheard a little White boy standing next to his mother in front of me in the supermarket check-out line ask four-year-old Morgan loudly, "Are you Black or are you White?"

Morgan just stared as he belligerently stood nose to nose with her.

"Are you *Black*...or are you *White*?" he yelled insistently again, as I grabbed her hand and hastily exited the store.

Here was the moment of truth. I had never considered what to say to her about this and had somehow avoided facing the fact that I would have to be prepared to do so while she was still so young. Since birth, she had been surrounded by nearly as many African-Americans as White people. She was certainly aware of who her father was. Further, she had spent nearly two months at one point living with her dad at his sister's house in another city, so she knew that she had an entire Black family of aunts and uncles and cousins who had embraced her as one of their own. I guess I thought she would just get it by osmosis. But her stare in the grocery store said otherwise.

I flashed back to the moment when an attractive young professional-looking African-American woman railed loudly at me from behind an information table at the Black Family Conference I had attended when seven months pregnant with my daughter. I had confided in her, in a bid for acceptance, I suppose, that the child I carried was Black. Without a moment's hesitation, she went ballistic.

"What you have done is *wrong*!" she shouted at me, drawing attention from people in all directions, much to my embarrassment. "You will *never* be able to give this baby what it needs as a Black child!"

Quickly recovering from my shock, I leaned across the corner of the table, looking dead into her eyes, and said pointedly, but for her ears alone, "You may not agree with what I've done, but there are *lots* of us out here doing it, and we're not going *anywhere*. So you'd better come to grips with it, whether you like it or not." Still, here I was, four years later, about to find out how right she might have been.

I began my presentation to Morgan even before we got home. Driving down the street, I said to her, "Morgan, you know that your father is Black and I am White. That means that you are both races. Now some people say that if you have *any* Black in your father's *or* your mother's family, you are automatically Black yourself. But, regardless, they're going to eventually expect you to decide and declare what you consider yourself –Black or White or what." It was the best I could do for a beginning on such short notice.

"That's stupid," she stated flatly.

"I know that," I replied, "but that's the way it is."

When we got home, I started at the beginning of the historical evolution of the concept of "race."

"Originally, most Black people lived in Africa," I began. "They had a long history of greatness. They were doing brain-surgery when Europeans were still peeping out of caves in animal skins and living in the Dark Ages. Way back then, Africans already had libraries with millions of scrolls. They built the Sphinx and the Pyramids. They lived in lands that had great riches and they passed down knowledge and skills from generation to generation for hundreds and even thousands of years. They saw all life as sacred, not just human life."

Inside my head, I was trying to pick and choose among the many things I had learned to find just the right ones to share with this little girl who was standing on the other side of the dining table like an animal frozen in headlights, listening to me, her mother and now her teacher of racial wisdom. The weight of the responsibility of the moment was threatening to flatten my brain. This was my baby, my beautiful child, who captured the hearts of everyone who saw her, who had said to me one day as I questioned her multi-colored outfit, "I don't just want to look like some 'cute person.' I want to look like my *Self*!" How could I possibly rise to the formidable challenge of telling her the truth without shattering her faith in life, in me (her White mother), in herself?

I continued. "Then, the Europeans decided they needed more riches, so they went to Africa and snatched millions of Africans away from their families and their homes and their land and carried them away on boats to be slaves in North America where the United States is now, where we live. Many, many Africans died horrible deaths before the boats ever even got here. And when the Africans did get here, the White people wouldn't let the Africans use their real names or their own languages or worship in their own way or marry each other or even keep their own children. The White people forced these African slaves to work very, very, very hard and they never let them go until they died."

Morgan and I were now locked in history, our eyes hardly blinking as we stared into each other's faces. And she was taking almost imperceptible little steps around the edge of the table, slowly, slowly coming toward her mother.

"Then one day," I went on, "there was a great war where many men died to decide whether or not the Africans in the United States would be slaves or be free people. And when the war was over, the side that fought to free the slaves won, so the Africans were freed."

At this point, Morgan backed up and slid into my lap, no longer looking at me, but still listening as though the life of her young psyche depended on it.

"Still," I couldn't look at her either as I continued, "some White people think that they're better than Black people, and because of that, they do bad things sometimes. So Black people and White people have to work together to change the way our society is. That's how your daddy and I got together and that's how you were born. You're Black *and* White and *beautiful* and *smart* and you have the strength and the power of great people inside you."

I was emotionally exhausted and had run out of words, but it didn't matter because Morgan had her own thoughts. "You're one of the *good* White people, Mom," she said, looking up at me finally from over her shoulder.

"That's high praise," I said to my beautiful, Black child, "coming from you."

---

[i] Pp 78-104 in Black Fire: An Anthology of Afro-American Writing edited by Amiri Baraka and Larry Neal (Black Classic Press, 2007).

Becky Hensley makes the grade

Q-C STYLE

From welfare mom to college graduate — in just one year!

Becky Hensley

PART THREE

1987

It was the first week of August in 1987 when I received a phone call from the Sociology Department graduate student advisor at Western Illinois University asking me did I want to come to Macomb, ninety miles away, to enter graduate school. I had only just finished my last test at the undergraduate level through the WIU branch where I lived, and I had written a one paragraph letter asking whether or not it might be possible for me to get an assistantship in sociology sometime in the following year.

I was not absolutely certain what sociology was, but Calvin was a sociologist and he seemed to study people and then write about them, something I had been doing for years as a journalist, so I thought it might be a good fit. My plan, of sorts, was to specialize in criminal justice and become an "expert witness" in court cases. I imagined that it would be possible that way for me to be useful, and maybe even important, in a field I already knew something about.

I had entered a non-traditional degree program through WIU the year before and, while working full-time as a public aide caseworker and taking night classes, I had compiled a 705-page portfolio that resulted in my being awarded a total of fifty-six college credits by eleven professors who believed that I had learned through experience what they would have taught me in their courses. This was a dazzling enough feat to have gotten my photo into the local newspaper next to an article with a headline reading, "From Welfare Mom To College Grad In Just One Year!" But I didn't know about the GRE, a special exam required for admittance to most graduate schools and, in fact, could not even document a grade point average because I had received so many of my credits by sitting for College Level Examination Program tests, compiling the portfolio, and so on. Nevertheless, the advisor informed me, I would be admitted conditionally if I could present myself for classes in only two weeks. I was being offered an assistantship of only $400 per month, had never even seen the campus or the town before, and knew not one living soul in the community. I agreed immediately to come, hung up the phone, and gave my supervisor my two weeks' notice.

Sixteen days later, the day after my last day at work, I packed up my car and my soon-to-be-ex-boyfriend's van with what little I had worth taking with me and moved to Macomb with Morgan and Eli in tow. On the Saturday midway between my giving notice and our move, I had driven to Macomb and signed the lease on a shabby little house a block from the campus. It had only two bedrooms, so I was to sleep in the dining room behind a curtain, a lack of privacy that none of us was used to. And the rent was $200 per month, which meant that all of our other expenses would have to be covered by the remaining half of my assistantship, plus food stamps, of course, and student loans, but my tuition was paid as part of my assistantship and I had lived on less, so I felt like it wasn't going to be a problem.

Nevertheless, when my father commented casually that he really couldn't understand why I would leave secure employment with the state and a stable home to go off and put myself in a position where I wasn't even sure how I was going to feed my children, I burst into tears and ranted until he hugged me to shut me up.

I wasn't sure myself why I was doing this thing, but I had expected my undergraduate degree to take several years to achieve and my momentum was up, so it seemed appropriate somehow to just keep going. In truth, I hadn't expected the possibility of graduate school to present itself so quickly. When I learned a little more about higher education, I realized that what had happened was that a potential student who had originally accepted the assistantship had withdrawn their acceptance at the last minute, leaving the funds uncommitted. This was a problem for the department in that uncommitted funding could result the subsequent year in the department's budget being cut by that amount if it was deemed unnecessary.

So the WIU Sociology Department pundits really had nothing to lose if I flunked out half way through my first semester. By that time, their funding levels for the next year would be safe, which was infinitely more important to them in the long run than whether or not I distinguished myself as a scholar. And I was willing to step in at the last minute, which is exactly what they needed.

On the other hand, here was my golden opportunity to prove myself — to myself, if no one else — because with a non-traditional bachelor's degree in liberal arts and no GRE score or grade point average, I probably wouldn't have been able to get into any other graduate school in the nation at that point. But I was duly enrolled at WIU and had begun graduate level classes before I even officially received my undergraduate diploma in the mail. It should have been a red-letter day. I was a 41-year-old White woman from the mountains of Kentucky with two children, one of which was bi-racial, and had just come off of five years on welfare. But I was far too busy to celebrate.

Within two weeks, I realized that what I already knew about the criminal justice system was light years ahead of what was being discussed and written about in academic circles. Making *that* my specialization would rapidly reduce me to beating my head against the same brick wall with which I had become so familiar while I was with the National Prison Center and the Church of the New Song. So before going to bed one night, I asked myself, "If I could affect one area of interest in the United States today, what would that area be?" And I knew immediately that the answer was "race."

* * *

When I first saw the little house I had rented the month before, the former occupants, who happened to be an African couple from Botswana, were still there. They introduced themselves as Reginald and Mmone Ketshabile and, typical of people from many African cultures, they were warmly hospitable in spite of the imposition of the presence of a stranger in their home while they were trying to prepare to move into housing on the campus. It was a very propitious meeting for me, as I took the opportunity to cement the relationship with my first friends in Macomb and my first African friends ever.

"Don't forget me," I pressed them urgently that afternoon. "I don't know *anyone*, and I will need friends..." What I didn't realize at the time was that United States citizens don't typically make such an effort to befriend international students, particularly those from Africa.

Reginald and Mmone assured me that they would not leave me abandoned and they didn't. Shortly after the beginning of the semester, they dropped by one afternoon for a visit, inviting me to come over to see their new apartment on campus, which I did. And this was the start of a love affair between myself and the African student community in Macomb.

In an attempt to carve out a special niche for itself among the cadre of public universities in the state, Western Illinois University had decided to actively recruit international students. Consequently, nearly one-third of Western's twelve thousand students at that time were from some other country than the United States. It was glorious. All manner of dress in various combinations could be seen on any given day when walking across the campus. Multiple velvet-sounding languages floated through the buildings between classes. And the library had an international tea room on the first floor where decadent desserts and specialty coffees and teas could be enjoyed in the afternoon while surrounded by the flags of many nations.

In no time, our house became a center of activity for people from all over the world. And soon, even Morgan could point out a half dozen countries on the big map of Africa on the wall of her room, chirping in her child's voice, "This is *Eritrea*, where Berhane is from, and this is *Sudan*, where Martin is from, and this is *Botswana*, where Reginald and Mmone are from..." I was sure that Morgan's baptism into racial consciousness would no longer be a problem.

"I'm Black *and* White," she would announce proudly to anyone who would listen. After she learned that all DNA had been traced back to "Lucy," a woman who lived in central-eastern Africa some ten thousand years ago or so, she became really incorrigible. "Where are *you* from?" she would ask an unsuspecting White American visitor. Then, no matter what they answered, she would correct them with,

"No, you're not! You're from *Africa!*" And she would dissolve into a fit of helpless giggles.

Nevertheless, there were still moments we could not escape. One afternoon, Morgan came home from day care, where she spent her afternoons while I was in classes, beside herself with frustration.

"The other kids won't believe that I'm an *American!*" she said stomping one foot. "They ask me where I'm from and I tell them and they won't *believe* me! They say I must be from some other *country!*"

She was almost in tears and I knew that there was no tidy answer to her dilemma. This was going to be something that she would be dealing with for the rest of her life, most of the time when I wouldn't be there to fix it. Apparently, the other children eventually lost interest in Morgan's appearance as a focal point because she never mentioned it again and I doubt that she even remembers it anymore, but then and now, the socially-constructed political notion of race demands that we label ourselves and each other, that we take our proper positions and own up to what we "are," or it will be done for us.

As the years went by, the questions never ceased.

"Is that your *real* mom or were you *adopted?*" some rank stranger might ask Morgan boldly, without any introduction. Or of me, they would demand to know, "Is that your *biological* child?" as if I owed them an explanation. It never failed to amaze me that children and even adults we did not know and did not invite would approach us in public as if we were freaks of nature, always on display and warranting no privacy. Children taught never to walk up and ask pointed questions of a person in a wheel chair would demand information about Morgan's lineage and my sexual practices as if we should welcome their interest and attention.

Morgan and Eli often appeared together in the neighborhoods where we lived. Finally one day they mentioned to me that they were routinely queried about whether or not they were really brother and sister. Then, they told me, once they had assured the questioner that they were, they would usually be asked, "Then why do you look so *different*?"

"And what do you *say* to that?" I asked gravely, showing a mother's concern for her young.

"That we had different *fathers*!" they blurted out at the same time, as if to say, "Of *course*!" It was a trying time for all of us, but they seemed to have the matter in hand.

The following year, when we moved to Tallahassee, Florida, so that I could continue my graduate studies at Florida State University, Eli took to wearing a "Free Africa" necklace he had been given by one of our African friends. Since Tallahassee had a long and illustrious history as a southern city and, indeed, was often referred to as "South Georgia" even by some of the people that lived there, I was afraid for my son and told him so.

"I'm afraid that somebody's going to hurt you," I admitted to him one afternoon when he was thirteen and had just started attending the middle school in our new city.

"Mom," came his immediate reply, "Nothing is *ever* going to change, if nobody's willing to get *hurt*." I was astonished by such a statement coming out of the mouth of someone I considered little more than a child, and I knew he was right, but I didn't want it to be any of us, regardless of my life choices.

In Macomb, Eli found big brothers, both White and Black, on the football team, in a house full of guys in the ROTC program, even a Black fraternity, the members of which told him that when he grew up they'd be proud to have him join, regardless of his race. I thought there was something magical about him. In truth, he was just being his mother's son. He went to his first International Festival in a stroller, and had been carried into restaurants by a Black man when he was only two. And his sister, who he not only loved very much, but felt very protective toward, was immediately visibly recognizable as a child of color.

For her eighth birthday, Eli wrote Morgan a poem:

> *Africa's child*
> *today, tomorrow*
> *never will change*
> *today, tomorrow*
> *black and proud*
> *today, tomorrow*
> *fight for power*
> *today, tomorrow*
> *black and white*
> *today, tomorrow*
> *When will tomorrow come?*

When I started teaching, Morgan enjoyed coming with me to the classroom on occasion. She was bright and never intimidated by the young adults who were my students and who sometimes engaged her in conversations before and after class. One day, she came to me at home and said, "*I* want to take a sociology exam. Give *me* a question to answer."

I was charmed, of course, and set about immediately to create an "exam" for her on a yellow legal pad. "Why do people do the things they do?" I printed across the top of the sheet in letters she would be able to read. I wanted to make the question sociological because she had sat in on enough classes to know the difference, but I wanted to make it broad enough that she would be able to write about anything she wanted to and thus feel satisfied with the process and successful in her endeavor.

She took the pen and paper from me silently, retreated to the table where we usually ate our meals, and proceeded to fill the rest of the page with words, some of which were misspelled and some of which were written over because of mistakes she couldn't erase. When I read it, I was amazed. This little girl whose life was basically as good as a child's life can be and whose sunny disposition often made her a favorite among both adults and children wherever she went had written:

> *"I think Whites do the things they do to Black because Whites want to be better than Blacks and most Whites want to be better than all colored people. Whites think they are the king and queen of the world. I think Whites and Black should have the same rights and should be abel to do the same things. Whites treat other colored people like they are animals. I think it should be stop right now. Blacks should be respected just as Whites are and the same for all the other colored people."*

I was stunned. To this day, I have never heard her say anything this aggressive again, but I know it's in there because it was already in there when she was that young, and things in the United States are pretty much the same as they were then.

In Macomb, all three of us had friends of all types and it seemed utterly natural in that setting. Most of the international students lived on campus where apartments were small and parties were frowned on. So, after a while, it was not uncommon for me to be approached by a fellow graduate student who might say, "My cousin is going to be visiting this week-end from Mali and we're going to have a party."

"Great!" I would reply. "Where is it going to be?"

"Well, we were hoping to have it at your house," would come the answer. And we would laugh and set the date and time.

Before the party started, we would always pour a libation of wine or beer on the ground in memory of those who could not be with us, and then we would proceed to laugh and eat and talk and dance till the wee hours. And in the morning, I would find left-over beer and orange sodas in the refrigerator, the sodas being left by the Muslim students who wouldn't drink alcohol, but who would surely dance as long as the music was playing. When I graduated with my Master's degree, there were nearly thirty countries represented at the party and I knew that for me, this probably represented some kind of personal best and, undoubtedly, the end of an era in my life.

Under these circumstances, it was not surprising that, when I noticed a certain antagonism between Africans and African-Americans among my friends and acquaintances, I would eventually decide that here was something I wanted to learn more about. So I made the study my Master's thesis and entitled it, "Social Distance Between Africans and Black Americans and the Attitudes of White Americans Toward Both Groups."

When I would mention the topic to someone, they would sometimes raise what they saw as an obvious question. "Why should Africans and African-Americans feel positive toward each other? They have nothing in common. African-Americans were born *here*, after all, not in Africa." And I would explain that what interested me was not why there wasn't a positive relationship between Africans and African-Americans, but rather why they demonstrated such negativism toward each other.

"Individual members of each group call members of the other group 'arrogant.'" I would explain. "I can understand how people of Polish descent, for example, born in the United States, might not necessarily feel particularly positive toward Poland and the people there. In fact, many U.S. citizens take little interest in their ancestral backgrounds at all. But that doesn't explain why members of a group born in the U.S. would express *antagonism* toward people from their family's place of origin."

"And many Africans see what they consider to be a few flaws in U.S. culture overall," I would go on, "but they *often* express severe negativism toward Black Americans specifically. There's something going on here and I'd like to try to figure out what."

I proceeded to do all the social scientific back-flips required to conduct serious research. I turned the casual conversations into in-depth interviews which gave birth to a survey using a questionnaire, followed by group discussions to better understand the resistance I received when I tried to gather information on the topic from African-Americans.

The questionnaire asked first how close the person filling it out felt to groups other than their own. Secondly, it asked questions about how much and what kind of contact they had with Africans (if they were African-Americans) or African-Americans (if they were Africans). Next, it asked the person to describe Africans, Black Americans, and White Americans using adjectives from a list. Finally, it asked whether the writer preferred the term "African-American" or "Black American," and what Africa meant to them. It was an ambitious questionnaire. But I wasn't just an academic in an ivory tower asking dispassionate questions to create endless uninteresting statistics. I was rabidly curious. I loved all these people and I wanted to understand.

To first establish a benchmark related to the attitudes of White students on the campus toward African-American students, I decided to conduct two in-depth interviews with

White men just completing degrees in sociology. They were both happily married. They had both been successful in school and had good jobs waiting. Plus they both knew me and knew my perspectives on race. I figured they would bend over backward not to look racist, even if they were. That way, I felt I could assume that, whatever attitude they demonstrated would probably be a good indication of the *best* of what I might find in the overall White student body. I had a serious surprise coming.

An old sociological ploy is to ask the person being interviewed what other people like him or her seem to think. That way the interviewee can say things that might make them uncomfortable to admit about themselves. So I asked the younger of the two sociologists, who was finishing his Bachelor's degree, what he thought the general attitude of White students at WIU was toward Black American students.

"That they're not interested in studies," he responded. "That they get a free ride and don't even try. That they get financial aid and everything handed to them. Like, our parents *worked* to get what we have, but *theirs* are on welfare. So why don't they just leave it all to somebody who *wants* an education?"

I was puzzled at what the young man had said because many of the African-American students at Western were from affluent families in Chicago and clearly reflected that in their clothes, jewelry, and cars. But when I interviewed the other White student, who was finishing his Master's degree, I was stupefied. He started out slowly, but by the time he reached his finishing remarks, his face was blood-red and the veins were standing out in his forehead.

"I'm all *for* Black pride," he asserted, "but not at White *expense*—and the two seem to be interconnected. Black people and White people are wanting to stay on two different sides of the street now. You know, one of my relatives tells a joke about how you can take the nigger out of the *jungle,* but you can't take the jungle out of the *nigger*...Maybe it was a mistake to bring 'em here in the *first* place!"

I was absolutely flabbergasted. I didn't comment, but simply nodded, controlling my facial expression for all I was worth, and writing down his exact words, more sure than ever, now, that my thesis was going to kick ass. If these attitudes reflected what a couple of successful, young, White male *sociologists* felt about race when they were holding back because of my note-taking, I thought to myself, just **imagine** what the average old run-of-the-mill White man or woman might have lurking in *their* minds.

To make matters worse, people in the United States — Black *and* White — are inundated with information about Africa that makes it look as if most Africans live in trees and hunt their dinner with spears, which is patently untrue since many Africans now live in big cities just like the people in the rest of the world. On top of this, we learn almost nothing about African history in school, despite the fact that it is the biggest continent in the world and has been populated for thousands of years by multiple, highly-developed civilizations.

Consequently, in spite of the fact that most of the Africans on the WIU campus frequently out-dressed the other students in European fashions, spoke impeccable (though accented) English, and practiced the gracious manners of highly cosmopolitan people, the African-American students looked down on them. To make matters worse, most of the African-American students appeared to carry a concern that they would be "lumped in" with people that they described as "uncivilized, uneducated, and diseased," so they distanced themselves as greatly and in as many ways as possible.

The Africans, on the other hand, had been treated in their home countries to media portrayals of Black Americans in both news stories and movies as violent, drug-dealing gang-bangers. While this is true of some African-Americans, it is also true of some White Americans, some Asian-Americans, some Latino-Americans, and probably even some Native Americans, although there are hardly enough of them left to be sure. The point is that the images of African-Americans exported to Africa tended to be heavily skewed and presented to the exclusion of more positive or varied images. And this was compounded by the fact that Agency for International Development trainers in Washington, D.C., preparing the African students to go to their respective campuses, were reported by the Africans as telling them point blank not to room with Black Americans because they're violent and use drugs.

The result, of course, was that a Black American student and an African student could sit next to each other in a classroom in Macomb, Illinois, both speaking English, both taking the same course, both wearing jeans and Nikes, but calling each other "arrogant" because they were so cold toward each other. It was a classic scenario.

African-American students who were informed of the manipulation understood immediately. They deal with the issue of public image daily even in their own country.

One African student, asked what he thought was being accomplished by keeping the two groups from talking to each other, suggested, "When the White man comes to Africa, we treat him very, *very* well. We respect him *much*. If Africans really understood how badly the White man treats Black people in America, we might not *treat* him so well."

When I mentioned this statement to another young African who had only been in this country for a few months and asked him if he agreed with it, he exclaimed, "**Yes**! When I get home, I will **cane** White men in the **streets**!"

The completed thesis ran 103 pages long, not counting the bibliography and appendices, and when I made a presentation of my findings at the African Studies Association International Conference in Atlanta, Georgia, that fall, the hall, which was large, was jam-packed corner to corner. I didn't have the experience to realize what a thunderous introduction to the academic arena was indicated by a turn-out of this type. As soon as I finished and opened the floor for questions, though, a man of color in the center of the audience leapt to his feet as if he had been waiting impatiently for the opportunity and announced forcefully, "That is a **lie**!"

I was so taken aback by his emotional attack that I didn't really hear the rest of what he said, but I was absolutely confident that my findings were sound. I had checked and double-checked them against each other, the literature, history, and all manner of input from all manner of individual's experiences. It didn't matter that I didn't clearly get all his comments, though, because, even before he had finished them, another man of color stood and began to counter what the first man had said.

For the remaining duration of the conference, I was approached continually by academics from all over the world. Excited and even sometimes a little obsequious, they would hover at my elbow, grinning.

"You are very brave," they told me.

Their kudos reminded me of some lines from "Talk," a poem by the Russian poet Yevgeny Yevtushenko:

> *"How sharply our children will be ashamed*
> *taking at last their vengeance for these horrors*
> *remembering how in so strange a time*
> *common integrity could look like courage."*

* * *

While I was being molded into a sociologist, I began to mentally catalog my personal experiences and place them in the context of my new intellectual stance. There was no way to divorce my studies from my experiences anyway and, in fact, it was at Macomb that I began practices that I ultimately perfected later in Tallahassee and called "hanging out" and "being seen."

"Hanging out" made me comfortable in a range of milieus and made others comfortable with me, making it possible for me to receive more and more credible information about whatever I was trying to learn. "Being seen" had to do with what is often referred to as "being a regular" in a bar. One often has to "be seen" repeatedly and for an extended period before one is allowed to "hang out." In sociology, it turned out, these practices were called "participant observation."

I "hung out" with graduate students from other countries in Macomb. I "hung out" with poor, southern Black Americans in Tallahassee. And the consciousness that I had begun to develop in Morgan's early years, before studying sociology, blossomed during my two years in Macomb.

I remember one occasion that involved an invitation to a party that some enterprising young student had scotch-taped to an often-traveled campus sidewalk. I noticed the open invitation just as a young African-American woman going the other direction noticed it, as well. As we looked up from the sheet of paper, still walking without hesitation, our eyes connected, and in that brief moment, I realized that even though the invitation was an "open" one, the young, attractive student knew that it was not open to her.

I could actually feel her response to being shut out of an event unquestionably because she was "Black" — a social assignment she could not avoid — and I walked on, experiencing this new consciousness like a block of concrete shoved inside my head, the corners poking at the inside of my skull, the weight of it throwing me off balance, the bulk of it making it impossible to get rid of ever again. I have only to remember the incident and I can still see her eyes, like Reggie's, not accusing, but resigned and knowing and sad.

Invited to a party myself at the home of a Black woman professional married to a Nigerian economics professor at WIU, I went, excited at this opportunity to spend some time with people who had already scaled the walls I was studying. As I came down the stairs into the sunken living room, I had a chance to scan the faces of the others attending the party — either entirely or virtually entirely people of color — and they apparently had a chance to scan my face, as well.

Later that evening, when I was conversing with a Black American woman who was visiting from another city, she chuckled and admitted to me that she had already heard about me from her host, and that when I arrived, she had recognized me immediately because, watching me walk down the stairs, she could tell that I had been "shocked by the culture."

"Shocked by the culture?" I queried in response.

"Yes," she answered. "You know, 'shocked by the culture.' You've been touched by Blackness somehow and it shows."

"*Oh!*" I laughed, duly proud of myself for being construed by a total stranger as somehow bi-cultural in my orientation. The sociologist in me wanted to know precisely what "shocked by the culture" looks like to an African-American viewer. The street-wise bi-cultural part of me knew that it isn't something you can describe, but is rather perceived on the same level that recognizes danger in an otherwise blank White face.

* * *

A monumental experience for me during this same period involved following a Sudanese man to Toronto for a visit. He had had to leave the United States for Canada unexpectedly because he was from southern Sudan and his country's Arabic government was seeking the aid of the U.S. government in returning him to his country, where it was unsafe for him to be. Canada had a different policy toward the situation in Sudan at that time, so he sought and was granted asylum there. He had literally had to run for his life.

When he invited me to come to Toronto, I was very excited. Here was an opportunity to "hang out" with Sudanese refugees, soaking up whatever I could about their extraordinary situation.

Unfortunately, there was a great deal that I should have taken into consideration in advance, but could not, simply because I did not really understand the setting I was about to enter. The southern Sudanese culture, made up of multiple tribal groups, was markedly patriarchal, for one thing, so a woman would have little interest for them short of whatever favors she could offer as a woman, and she would have no status in their presence at all, no matter where she was from. Worse, in retrospect, I suspect that most of the dozen or so Sudanese men I found myself surrounded by for eighteen days were probably suffering from some of the classic manifestations of post-traumatic stress disorder because they had been fighting a civil war for years, some of them since they were children.

Needless to say, it was a rigorous experience, at best. I was frequently ignored, frightened by aggressive outbursts between them, and, though many of them could speak some or even very good English, they chose to do so very seldom, so I rarely knew what was going on and spent most of my time isolated and uncomfortable. They probably spoke so little English because some of them could not speak it at all and they had much more consideration for each other than for some random White woman from the United States who would soon be gone.

The low point of my visit was an incident when one of the men threatened to set me on fire if I didn't have sex with him. I did not give him what he demanded, but he scared me terribly because, by the time this occurred, I was no longer sure that he wouldn't do it, regardless of what my common sense was telling me.

By the time I left Toronto, I was so glad to see the United States again that even the buses looked beautiful to me. I was delirious with joy to be back in Macomb. Then, a young White male, grinning, called out a sexually-explicit invitation to me as we passed each other in our cars. I became instantly and inordinately enraged, throwing my arm out the window of my car and shoving the middle finger of my left hand high in the air while I shouted loudly enough to be heard a considerable distance, "Fuck *you*!"

My emotion was so intense that it startled even me. I went home to hide until I could figure out what in the world that sudden, spontaneous reaction had been about. Reginald and Mmone came over to hear about my trip and we sat on the porch for several hours while I described my visit to Toronto and then told them about what had just happened earlier that afternoon. Eventually, we sorted it out.

While I was in Toronto, I often felt as if I was nothing. The Sudanese men I visited had routinely walked out on me in the middle of a sentence and, in fact, had acted as if I was totally inconsequential most of the time. For a middle-class White woman from the United States, who is used to the privilege afforded her race and socio-economic status, this was mind-bending. After only eighteen days of being dealt with in such a manner, of being solidly on the bottom instead of on the top, when I finally felt safe to do so, I exploded. What a revelation! We laughed about it, but with knowing nods. A White woman had had a graphic moment of clarity about social position and she would be unlikely to ever forget it.

PART FOUR

1989

My original visit to Tallahassee in 1989 had centered totally on Florida State University. It was May and the city was heavy with pink and yellow flowers and the smell of mold on ancient trees. The professors had been warm and inviting. And the students had wined and dined me, taking me to the beach and plying me with shrimp, while drunkenly discussing intellectual pursuits and telling me just enough secrets about the department that I could somehow imagine I knew what it would be like to be there.

The crucial information I ignored was Tallahassee's history. A couple of different people in Macomb, attempting to warn me, asked me pointedly if I had considered the fact that Tallahassee had been part of the segregated south until only a couple of decades before. I brushed them off, dismissing their comments as irrelevant. "Time has passed," I responded lightly, superficially confident, though I surely knew better, that Jim Crow had moved on and been forgotten or at least that I would be up to the challenge if that was not so. White people can pick and choose when to be conscious of race or when to be concerned about what they're conscious of.

"If it's really still that bad," I joked flippantly, "then maybe they need a little of what I'll bring to the community..."

Nobody told me that Tallahassee was home to 10,000 slaves when emancipation was announced. Nor did they mention that entire Black families there were still "on premises," employed as servants who actually lived with wealthy White families into the 1970s. Nobody admitted to me in advance that the Ku Klux Klan still appeared in public in their regalia in broad daylight on a regular basis. Nobody shared with me that students had taken over parts of FSU in the 1960s to protest racism on campus — a racism that wasn't far under the surface yet — or that a massive and successful boycott of the Tallahassee bus system had paralleled the more famous one in Montgomery, Alabama, in 1956. And nobody I knew in Macomb appeared to realize that the unrest in Tallahassee had been so pervasive and so demanding during that era that, ultimately, hundreds of decently-paid jobs requiring unskilled labor had been created out of thin air expressly for African-Americans. In fact, the maintenance department at FSU, for example, had been virtually turned over to the local Black community as a make-peace.

But after the move, I was in town less than a week when I saw for the first time a stooped and ancient Black man with his eyes on the ground and a bag over his shoulder, shuffling along in the weeds next to a highway. The image cut my heart like a knife. Suddenly, I couldn't help but notice the swamps full of oak trees hanging with Spanish moss and the slow southern accents and the racial divide apparent everywhere. The flowers were still there and the University, but now it seemed as if I could hear voices from the past, as well, spirits still hovering over the water between the trees, panting and crying through time for generations, chased without rest for hundreds of years. I was horrified.

"What have I *done*?" I asked myself. "How am I going to survive five years in this place?" What I should also have been considering was the effect it would have on Eli and, even more so, on Morgan. But I couldn't begin to think about them when I couldn't come to grips with the demons myself. Frantic with the realization that I had just moved into the belly of the beast, as it were, and could not now leave because I was locked into FSU as a means of support with no place else to go, I decided that I would use the opportunity to study "race" further.

Nevertheless, on a personal level, I started trying to connect with the African-American community, desperate to know and have them know that I was dissociating myself immediately from Tallahassee's system of racial norms.

"Where are the Black clubs in Tallahassee?" I would ask one of the University's maintenance men or an African-American postal worker or someone I met standing in line at the grocery store.

"Clubs?" they would respond politely. "There aren't any Black clubs in Tallahassee."

"Of *course*, there are," I would counter, good-naturedly, smiling my encouragement. "There *must* be."

But they would assure me that there were not. And by the time I had asked the question half dozen times of different Black people in different settings only to get exactly the same response, I knew I was going to have to try a different tack. So when my thesis topic resulted in my being invited to appear on a panel for the African Students Association, I was delighted.

Sure enough, after the presentation, an African graduate student asked me for my phone number and subsequently invited me on a date. I chose my clothes carefully that night, putting on a dress and high heels, aware of how very visible I was going to be in this new community with its pretense of acceptance and its ties to the past.

As we stepped through the door into the darkness of the Embassy Club, an up-scale African-American establishment with multiple dance floors, several bars, and a rigid dress code, I immediately recognized one of the men I had queried about the existence of Black clubs in Tallahassee, but pretended not to see him. This was neither the time nor the place for me to act smart.

Over the next six months, I discovered two other popular dance clubs — small, loud with music, rough around the edges, and deep in Black neighborhoods. The first was near Florida A & M University. The crowd was younger and rowdier. It felt more dangerous to me and therefore less interesting. I was in my early forties, after all, though I looked as if I might be as much as a decade younger and got a great deal of attention with which I wasn't always entirely comfortable.

"I'm not too old for you," I would smile softly at men in their twenties in the smoky darkness. "You're too young for me."

"Age ain't nuthin' but a number," they would respond seductively. But I knew that they would be more trouble than they were worth, generally speaking, and I had long since learned how to leave the party before angry words started or the fists started flying.

The second neighborhood bar I discovered was jammed into a tiny little concrete block building painted white in the middle of a Black neighborhood populated by working poor, welfare recipients, and the elderly, sometimes all in the same house. It was relatively near where I lived, perched on a brightly lit corner with adequate parking, and almost always full beyond capacity with Black folks ready to dance.

An FSU maintenance man nicknamed "Kill Pretty" had introduced me to this club one night when I had dropped enough information that he could tell that I was going to be a "regular" with him or without him, and it rapidly became my party spot of choice. Every couple of weeks, I would put on my skin-tight jeans and my Laura Biagiotti wrap-around glasses and head for "the hood."

I was edgy about this place. I knew few of the people who hung out there, for one thing, but much more important was the fact that I was working on a Ph.D. now. I was soon teaching at both FSU and the local community college. I was a single mother of two young people who seemed to be requiring more, not less, attention as time went by. And I was feeling increasingly distant in my soul from the milieu surrounding what had until a couple of years before been my own life-style. But I wasn't willing or able to let it go as yet. The opportunity to dance till I sweated in the middle of a bunch of other people doing the same thing to music that put my brain in a trance was not only more than I could resist, it was something I needed in my life, even if I sometimes felt afraid.

In actuality, not only did I never experience anything negative in all my visits to this club, but I never saw anyone else having a negative experience there. The D.J., who wore a fly fedora, was "old school," the music was hot, and everybody in attendance always seemed to be there for the same reason I was.

One night, after I had entered the club and ordered a beer, I was approached at the bar, which only had about six stools, by an African-American man in a suit who slid up next to me and said in an oily voice, "I have a Bachelor's

Degree and a job as a professional at..." and he named some company or other with which I was not familiar.

I wasn't impressed. Looking at him flat-faced, I asked without smiling, "Then what are you doing in *here*?" And he disappeared into the jostling crowd. It was this kind of mentality that stood me in good stead in Black clubs.

Eventually, when I had reached a point that I would enter the Embassy Club alone at 11:30 on a Saturday night, I walked in, sat down at one of the bars, and ordered as if I didn't realize that I was the only White person in the place. The Black woman sitting next to me waited only a few moments before asking me point-blank, with an incredulous look on her face, "Aren't you *scared*?"

I laughed.

"I've been doing this for so long, I don't even think about it anymore," I answered.

"Well, you've got *nerve*," she decided, and proceeded for the rest of the night to give me inside information by signaling me with a "yes" or "no" when I was approached by men for a dance.

The fact is that I *was* scared. Always. Most sensibly, most of the time. And I let my fear inform my decisions about where to go, how to carry myself, who to talk with, and a range of other related matters. I always drove my own car. I always parked in a lighted area. I never looked at a man who was with another woman. I never danced with a man who looked down when I asked him if there was anyone *anywhere* who would be angry if I danced with him. I looked both women and men directly in the eyes when I spoke to them. I always spoke to the woman when both genders were present. I never made an undue spectacle of myself on the dance floor. And I slipped Black vernacular into my conversation with such frequency that, invariably, my conversational partner would be brought at some point to ask, "Where are you *from*?"

"You mean, where did I learn to *talk* like this?" I would respond, grinning, and then follow up with some vague reference to having lived many places. Ray had told me years before with a laugh after he listened to me talking on the telephone to one of my Black girlfriends on the other end of the line, "You've really *done* it! You can actually sound *Black*!"

After I had been in Tallahassee for about a year, Earline, a woman I met in a surplus cheese line, took me to a club out in the country. She only invited me, I felt sure, in spite of the fact that we had become friends over time, because I had a car and she did not. But, without her along, I would never have found it in a hundred years. It was a serious old-timey southern juke joint, perched in the middle of nowhere, with colored lanterns hanging from the trees and reflected in the finish of the cars parked precariously around it, the smell of barbeque and weed wafting into the car windows when we drove up.

Though I only went once, forever after that I could score immediate points with Black people in Tallahassee by finding a way to mention having been out there.

"How did you get to the *Midway*?" they would ask, with a sly grin and raised eyebrows, duly impressed. I didn't even need to prove it. The fact that I *knew* about the club was enough.

On the drive out, which took a half hour or so, Earline told me stories about her family. The one I remember best was about several of her uncles who had once beaten up one of the White insurance men that went door to door "back in the day" bilking Black folks out of their pennies on payday with promises of a decent burial which might or might not ever occur. This particular insurance man had somehow offended the brothers and, after beating him, they tied him up and put his head on the railroad tracks, leaving him there to die.

I recalled, as she told me the story, that Malcolm X's minister father was murdered the same way for supporting Marcus Garvey from his pulpit, but the incident was determined to be a suicide by the insurance company to which he had paid premiums for years before his death. Malcolm's mother, who eventually died in an insane asylum, was left without any form of income to support her family and so lost her five children to the foster care system, where Malcolm was soon instructed that being a lawyer was not "a reasonable goal for a colored boy."

I salted away the story about Earline's uncles in a new mental file I had begun to keep on the resistance of people of color to the system of racist oppression that has so prescribed and still prescribes their lives. It is interesting to note that Whites, who spend a great deal of energy being afraid of African-Americans, never like to think about why they are, in fact, afraid, why they countenance continued police brutality against African-Americans under dubious circumstances, and why they punish with such wild abandon any action on the part of a Black person, especially a Black man, against one of their own.

"The practice of slavery in the United States was a long time ago," Whites are quick to point out. "It doesn't have anything to do with the present, and certainly not *my* present, since *I* never held a slave."

"Besides," they will continue, "there has always been slavery and even Africans enslaved other Africans to sell to the Europeans, so why should *I* feel responsible for it?"

The answer is patent. We have been carefully taught, socialized, and instructed to see things from a very self-centered and specifically Euro-centric perspective. Yes,

Africans enslaved other Africans, and Greeks and Romans enslaved everybody, including each other and themselves. But there was a ghastly difference about the Triangular Trade, which was developed by Europe's embrace of capitalism.

Prior to capitalism, most of the European population was destitute and what accumulation of wealth there was had to do predominately with establishing and maintaining positions of power. A royal house without a room full of gold was literally unable to protect itself from encroaching enemies, some of whom might have been allies until the gold ran out.

Capitalism, which burst like a monster child out of the birth canal of the Industrial Revolution, introduced the idea of accumulating profit ("capital") for its own sake. Whereas previously, commodities (like grain or wool) would be sold to gain funds to buy other commodities (like horses or weaponry), capitalism was all about producing commodities not to acquire other commodities, but to create profit, to stockpile cash. Money became more important than life. And investment capital became king.

As West Africa entered a period of political and religious unrest, during which multiple ethnic and religious groups jockeyed for position, European opportunists were happy to offer funds or gun powder to swing the balance of power to the side of the most brutal or the most afraid. It was soon established that a very small investment could bankroll a ship to pick up slaves at gunpoint in West Africa and transfer them under horrific conditions to ports in the Western Hemisphere at a huge financial return. The empty ships could then be re-loaded in the "New World" with cotton, tobacco, coffee, and sugar, to be sold in hungry European markets and the profit re-invested in industrial factories — and more slave ships.

Ships began moving day and night from Europe to Africa to the colonies in the West and back to Europe like a conveyor belt through hell. Estimates suggest that as many as thirty to fifty million Africans died in the process of being delivered to the ports of call that awaited them, but since the initial investments were very small and the sheer numbers of bodies unfathomable, this in no way discouraged investors.

In fact, the British South Sea Company, created for the express purpose of transporting enslaved Africans, had among its shareholders most of the members of Parliament; the leading physical scientist, Sir Isaac Newton; major authors Jonathan Swift and Daniel Defoe; and even the Earl of Halifax, who founded the Bank of England. So it was not remarkable that in the British colony that became the United States, early leaders, including its first six Presidents were slave holders themselves. George Washington, famous for his dentures, had them made, it has now been suggested, not from wood, as was previously reported, but from teeth extracted from the mouths of his living slaves.

Once the enslaved Africans were brought to the Western Hemisphere, they were stripped of every grace ordinarily afforded humans in a rational society. The nexus at which point the peculiar institution of slavery met the new capitalistic institution of private ownership wherein the bottom line was always short-term profit, regardless of moral implications, produced a nightmare of unprecedented proportions for people of color.

The results were utterly predictable. Major slave up-risings averaged one per year from the very beginning of the enterprise and even White men, like John Brown, led or joined violent attacks against brutal masters and an even more brutal system. Advertisements for run-away slaves were in nearly every newspaper and posted all over the country, listing identifiers that were heinous reminders of previous attempts to escape: scars, brands, and missing body parts, as if these did not indict the masters more than the humans running for their very lives.

Letters and diaries from the period describe in quiet tension the continual blanket of fear that plagued the White community throughout the south. Valerie Martin's novel entitled Property graphically presents a White southern mindset unable to imagine what a person could be thinking who would treat people of African descent as ordinary humans. Nevertheless, intellectual oblivion notwithstanding, many Whites considered Black people, slave or free, dangerous to them — for good reason — and maintained a vicious vigilance to "keep them in their place."

It is not a mistake that keeping African-Americans "in their place" was a primary statement of racist purpose by many Whites during the struggle for civil rights in the 1960s, long after slave ships were not allowed to dock in the United States, long after the Civil War, and long after the Emancipation Proclamation. All the social institutions in the United States to the present were established and have been continually maintained by a White power structure committed to the making of money for those who have most benefited from that power structure being in place. This is hardly news to people of color. And the pretense of being asleep about the matter so prevalent in White society in this country is not new either.

It is at least partly that urgent need to pretend not to know or not to notice that makes White fear so evident. Like a two-year-old with her hands over her eyes, chanting over and over, "You can't *see* me! You can't *see* me!" White people seem to imagine that, if they don't recognize the continual barrage of White Supremacy that free-floats throughout our daily lives, constantly working to crush the bodies, souls, and spirits of people of color, African-Americans won't be able to hold them responsible. The idea is about as silly, ultimately, as the two-year-old's chant.

But as Amiri Baraka wrote fifty years ago:

> *"Most White men I meet say they are not responsible. Perhaps it is best to be left there. To take them at their word, that I'm hip, you are not responsible to the world. But you will be held responsible, anyway, since you own it, you think."*[i]

The fear can be painfully debilitating to African-American men who just want to be able to walk down the street in peace without having to feel that they are being perceived as bogeymen on every side, and without having to worry that they may, at any moment, become a victim themselves of White attitudes toward and about them. But it can also be a joke to those who have been forced to learn to laugh at it to maintain any sanity at all.

A Black man who did time in the Florida state correctional system years ago explained to me once that what used to be called the Raiford State Penitentiary East Unit was reserved for men who were classified as so hard core and incorrigible that they had to be separated from the rest of the population. Consequently, even years later, when a man who knew this wanted to scare someone, he'd "put a little Eas' on it." He'd strike a stance and don a facial expression characteristically guaranteed to put the fear of God into his opponent. It was conscious. He'd know he was doing it. He was practicing the art. And he knew the effect it would have.

This particular man, who ordinarily carried himself in a very non-assuming manner, went on to tell me a story about how, when he was younger, he or one of his friends would sometimes, as a joke, he said, stroll up to a White businessman sitting in his car in a parking lot and simply bark — puttin' a little Eas' on it — "Gimme two dollars!" Invariably, my friend reported, the victim would panic and whip out some money immediately, offering it through the window with a shaking hand. The man telling the story could hardly contain himself as he regaled the terrified reaction of the poor businessman. He said it was sometimes hard not to burst out laughing even as the "joke" was being played.

The point is that this man was not acting out of meanness, but out of being so hurt and so fed up with a system committed to portraying him as a brute monster, that he finally resorted to *playing* that monster as a form of payback and momentary relief. For White Americans in 2015 to keep pretending that they will not and should not have to acknowledge the rage of people of color who have been suffering White stupidity, cruelty, and privilege for five hundred years suggests a flaw in judgment that will deserve whatever it gets. No people have ever allowed themselves to be oppressed forever. African-Americans resisted White domination in the 1600s, in the 1700s, in the 1800s, in the 1900s, and will resist that domination until it no longer exists or until this country has been brought to its knees by the rigid idiocy of its commitment to White Supremacist power.

When the Kerner Commission — a body made up almost entirely of White men — reported in 1968 that the United States was moving toward becoming, "two nations, one Black and one White, separate and unequal,"[ii] it was not reporting something that the population of this country did not know. It was reporting something that its White citizens did not want to admit or deal with, which is a long, long way from being the same thing.

Moreover, the Commission's suggestion that this was a process getting *worse*, it would seem to me, begged the question about exactly when it had gotten *better*. Were we moving toward becoming two nations in 1968, whereas before that, African-Americans operated more fully as equals in their daily lives as U.S. citizens? Nearly fifty years later, African-Americans are still being lynched, the African-American community experiences a rate of unemployment that is double that of White Americans, and African-Americans suffer 2-1/2 times the incidents of heart failure as their White counterparts. James Baldwin once said that all we ever need to know about race in America we can learn by asking a White man would he want to be Black.

African-Americans who are able to rise to any position in the face of these kinds of obstacles and odds are not demonstrating that the problem does not exist or that anyone of color can do it, but rather the indomitable courage of the human spirit. And when you consider that millions of African-Americans have distinguished themselves over the past five hundred years, regardless of the context in which they had to accomplish their triumphs — however large or small — it is truly, truly amazing. No wonder White people are afraid.

But no more afraid than African-Americans. After all, White Americans who created, benefit from, and continue to perpetuate this system of apartheid oppression against people of color in the United States are the ones with all the power. It would be enough to scare anybody. Especially anyone who has children. This is why I was stone-walled when I first arrived in Tallahassee. But I knew what to do about it, though it took some time.

* * *

Florida State's campus was ridiculously short on parking spaces. So, even though I had paid for a parking pass, I soon made it a practice to park on Mississippi Street[iii], which paralleled Tennessee Street, a main drag running through the city and forming one of the boundaries of FSU. Mississippi Street was one of a number of streets that comprised "Frenchtown," one of Tallahassee's oldest and poorest neighborhoods. It was no secret that the University longed to swallow it up someday and that Tallahassee as a city would not be sorry when it happened. But at this point, Frenchtown lay immediately next to the FSU campus, fully functional as a poor Black neighborhood, complete with a cracktown barely a block from the campus.

Many of the houses on Mississippi Street were wooden, old and small, with porches that rested on concrete blocks and skinny dogs barking from stakes in backyards lined with bushes and shaded by trees. Parking next to the curb on Mississippi Street and then walking to my building on the campus only took about ten minutes at most, so it was hardly an inconvenience, but nevertheless, there were many students who would not do it because they feared being accosted on their way back to their cars at night or having their cars broken into while they were gone.

Actually, once I had established myself as a "regular," residents of the block I always parked on would look out for me, even going so far as to call me at my office on a couple of occasions to inform me that I had locked my keys in my car and asking if I'd like them to remove the keys so that when I was done for the day, I could go home. But establishing myself as a regular took some doing.

I had parked in that block every day for at least six months without ever getting a single person to speak to me even when I spoke first. African-Americans in Tallahassee at that time had little desire to interact any more than they absolutely had to with White people. But I understood and just kept appearing, like a stray cat, every morning and every evening, until one morning, I was finally greeted by an 89-

year-old Black woman from the porch of a house marked by peeling paint and situated behind a wire fence.

"Do you have any candy?" she asked, getting straight to the point.

"No," I replied with respect, slowing down considerably, but not stopping because to stop might rouse someone's concern. "I don't."

"Well, then," she pressed further. "Do you have any Coca-Cola?"

I saw my opportunity and stopped walking, just as a young man came around the house from the backyard to intervene.

"Don't mind her," he urged politely, speaking quickly, attempting to avoid the possibility that I might feel offended in any way. "She's always asking everybody for candy and Coca-Cola. She doesn't know what she's doing."

"That's all right," I said congenially. "I don't mind." And then, turning to the elderly woman, I added, "I don't have any Coca-Cola right now, but when I come back later this afternoon, I promise you that I will bring you some then, okay?"

The woman nodded her agreement and when I returned seven hours later with a cold, 16-ounce bottle of Coca-Cola in my bag, she was vigilantly waiting in the swing on her porch and hurried out to meet me as I came up to the gate.

Her god-son, who turned out to be named Mervin, came through the screen door onto the porch as the exchange was being made. The elderly woman's grin split the aged wrinkles on her face and she retreated with her prize to the swing, where she took a deep swallow and exhaled a satisfied sigh.

"She loves sugar," he volunteered with an indulgent smile, picking up where he had left off that morning. "You a student at FSU?"

I replied that I was.

"I've seen you walk this way before," he admitted.

"Yeah," I agreed. "I usually park here because I'm a graduate student in sociology and my building is just on the other side of Tennessee Street."

We finished our conversation shortly and I moved on, but the contact had been made. Over the next five years, I saw a great deal of Mervin Green and his common-law wife, Jeanette, their nephew, Quincy, and Mervin's god-mother, Edna Swann, who Mervin pointedly instructed me to call "Miss Edna," out of respect for her age. At least two days per week, one or more of them and I would sit for hours on their porch, sometimes into the evening, while Quincy swung on a tire hanging from a tree branch in the front yard or sat in my lap.

At the first of the month, we would drink a beer. Then, on one occasion, Morgan and I went to a barbeque in their backyard. And when their "yard dog," a chow, had a litter of pups by a Rottweiler from down the street, Morgan and I picked one out before its eyes were opened, naming it "Missie" in honor of the street where it was born, and taking it home a couple of months later. I took Mervin and Jeanette pecans from the tree behind my house. And I even took them Christmas presents one year. But they gave me infinitely more than that.

For one thing, if I intended to study race in Tallahassee, Mervin and Jeanette's porch was a great spot to begin and a serious reference point to return to when I lost my bearings. Through them, I met several other families and individuals in that block. And sitting on their porch, sipping beer and watching fire flies, I heard many things that White folks don't often hear.

Before I started hearing much, however, Mervin took the time to tell me a story one day. He was very serious when he related the tale and did not explain in so many words why he was telling it, but it was a story about a bird that initially led an enemy away from its nest and eventually wound up losing its life when it decided to trust the enemy. The best I could figure out, he was asking me to be careful with him and his little family, to respect them and understand that he expected me to honor that respect and not put them in some kind of vague danger for having trusted me.

"You understand what I'm sayin'?" he queried when he was through.

And I assured him gravely that I did. I walked away from him that day feeling that Mervin and I were equals. I might be working on a Ph.D., but Mervin, who couldn't read more than a few letters, was one smart cookie. In time, I learned that Mervin had been in foster care as a child, but had started earning money when he was just a boy. By the time he was fourteen, he owned two cars and a horse and was making so much money that the state had pushed him out of the home they were providing and stopped supporting him altogether, saying that he could support himself.

A White man for whom he had worked for fourteen years convinced Mervin that he had no need to finish school, since he had a good job. And Mervin had always understood that if you worked for someone for twenty years, you could then retire with a pension, so he listened to the man and quit school.

But when the man sold his business to a corporation and was presented with the dilemma of suggesting which of his two employees they should keep, he recommended the White man he had hired years after he hired Mervin. Mervin believed that this was a perfect example of why a person of color should never entirely trust a White person, no matter how nice they seem or how long they have known them. And now, at least for the time being, he was unemployed and looking after Miss Edna.

This turned out to be a recurring theme among low income Black people in Tallahassee. Many of them had to and thought nothing of working two or even three jobs at the same time, assuming they could get one at all. "Kill Pretty," for example, worked from 5:00 a.m. to 2:00 p.m. at FSU, went to a second job at the hospital after that every day, and had a collection of hogs out in the country somewhere that he was raising as a side line. His old Ford truck, with its dents, rust, and patchy paint job, looked inconsequential until he revved the motor and took off at a stop light one day, leaving the other vehicles in his dust with their drivers startled.

"I had this baby custom-made," he joked. "It takes a *long* time to make a truck look this bad with this much power under the hood."

Earline worked very hard as an L.P.N., dragging home exhausted, but she was making $25 per hour plus shift incentives, over-time, and bonuses. I had absolutely no idea what she spent her money on, as her life-style was not at all ostentatious and she always seemed to be broke. She loved her son Ronnie and kept him dressed well, but I got the impression that Earline might have been serving as a piggy-bank for a number of hangers-on, including her mother, her step-father, and an ex-husband who used to beat her and then take her money, too.

And so I came to understood that just because an African-American man or woman in Tallahassee looked "country" didn't necessarily mean that they were destitute, although they might be. Soon, I was telling a joke about the difference between Black folks and White folks.

"*Black* folks," I would recount, "will tell you that they *don't* have any money, even if they *do*."

"*White* folks, on the other hand," I would continue, "will tell you that they *have* money when they *don't*."

Of course, it didn't matter how often I told African-Americans that I could barely afford fuel oil to heat my house. They all seemed to be absolutely certain that all White folks were rich and just didn't want anyone to know it. I would tell them my little joke and they would laugh, but when I repeated that I was just a poor student, they would shrug and shake their heads, and it was apparent that they were letting me say whatever I wanted, but I wasn't fooling *them*.

---

[i] Home by Amiri Baraka (NY: William Morrow and Co., Inc., 1966, p. 191)

[ii] The Report on the National Advisory Commission on Civil Disorders, Chair: Gov. Otto Kerner, Jr. of Illinois (2/29/68)

[iii] The name of this street has been changed to respect the privacy of the residents.

1990

Shortly after I arrived on the Florida State University campus, I sought out the Director of Black Studies, an African-American professor named Bill Jones. William T. Jones, was Harvard-trained and had taught Religious Studies at both Princeton and Yale before coming to FSU. His academic credentials were impeccable and he had all the appropriate publications, honors, awards, and distinctions, but his persona is what made Bill special. Higher education is an arena where the game is to appear humble, while not really being humble at all, but somewhere along the line, Bill rejected this practice in favor of being kind and caring and supportive and real. And he was brilliant.

I watched his secretary, who treated him like a god; I watched the young Black students who buzzed around the office like purposeful bees in a hive; and White as I was, I attached myself immediately to this man's entourage. Over time, I not only took his course on institutionalized oppression in social science methodology, but I would follow him around the campus, sitting in on his lectures even when

I wasn't enrolled in the class, carrying his briefcase and erasing his blackboards like an apprentice. I had a "major professor," Mike Armer, who was my advisor and safe haven in the Sociology Department, but Bill was my life coach and mentor at FSU and, even after he retired, I was still given to sitting at his feet whenever he would let me.

When my second summer on the campus approached and I needed a source of income for a couple of months, I went straight to Bill and he didn't let me down. He made a quick phone call and sent me over to be interviewed for a teaching slot with a program offering urban high school students from all over Florida — virtually all of whom were Black — a six-week summer residential experience on the campus. I had a good recommendation letter for the work I had done helping young African-American freshmen at Western Illinois University to make a smooth transition into college life, so the man that ran the program, in light of my background and in deference to Bill, I'm sure, just asked me what I could teach them that the young students might want to learn.

I told him I would think about it and call him with some suggestions, which I did. He listened and decided that I would teach "Between the Lines: African-American Experience as Literature." I wanted to craft it as something of a sociological/literary cross-over course and I was excited to put it together and present it. I gathered poems and non-fiction, autobiographical pieces, letters, stories, and even a few pages of Ntozake Shange's play, "Spell Number 7." It was a 145-page collection spanning more than two hundred years and included the kind of writers I hoped someday to introduce to Morgan. When I had exhausted my own favorites and researched at the library for other important contributions, I even called Calvin Hernton to ask for his input. You would have thought I was writing my dissertation and I didn't even know if my fifteen and sixteen-year-old students would get it.

They got it all right. We electrified each other. Rather than just throwing the material at them, I would read it to them aloud. With drama. With love. Stopping sometimes to explain something or make a comment or engage them in talk. In no time at all, we had changed each other for all time.

They told me about their lives: the fights they got into to protect themselves or their image, the difficulties they encountered with racist teachers, the concerns they felt for their parents who struggled so hard to support and encourage them and their younger siblings who appeared to them as more vulnerable versions of themselves. I was captured, and in a desire to offer them a gift they could take with them, I wrote a statement for them to read out loud when things at home got to be too much:

§

A Statement for People of African Descent

All my life, I have heard, read, and been surrounded by definitions of myself that were calculated to reduce my own opinion of who I am and prevent me from reaching the historical fulfillment of my whole personhood. I hereby and forever now reject these definitions, pledging to stand up and shine wherever I am, speaking the truth as I have experienced it, and working for justice for myself and my people.

Am I lazy? No! I am **not** lazy!

> *My heritage is one of hard work. It built the giant sphinx of Egypt, the golden palaces of Timbuktu, and the magnificent libraries of Songhay, before being forced across the Atlantic to build yet another civilization on yet*

another continent with hard, hard work. No matter how long the road, no matter how heavy the burden, my people have remained strong in the face of our struggles. And however tired and discouraged we may have felt, we have continued to work for the freedom of our people.

Am I ugly? No! I am **not** ugly!

My heritage is one of such extraordinary beauty that hunger, pain, and poverty cannot hide it, other cultural characteristics cannot mask it, and a history of hard work cannot erase it. The addition of my blood line strengthens and beautifies the human race wherever it is introduced. And people of other cultures seek to emulate the glow of the African appearance in its exotic diversity and its loveliness of composition.

Am I ignorant? No! I am **not** ignorant!

My heritage is one that filled monumental libraries, maintained complex and lengthy oral histories spanning multiple continents, and taught European sailors that oceans could be crossed. My people developed intricate poetic forms and used them spontaneously to suit the moment and the need, created works of art that bring awe to every viewer, and made music, art, beauty, and reason a part of the most commonplace human existence. My people made major contributions in every area of science and technology, continuing to do so even when not afforded the smallest recognitions.

Am I violent? No! I am **not** violent!

> *My heritage is one that, where less oppressed,
> appears much less violent than the so-called
> "more developed" cultures. My people have
> such a strong sense of social responsibility
> that even when we were approached so
> brutally in Africa, and even when we have
> continually and for such a long time been
> treated so mercilessly by our oppressors, we
> nevertheless have maintained our dignity, our
> spiritual consciousness, and our sense of the
> sacredness of all life, including our own. We
> have chosen not to respond to our oppressors
> in kind even when all of history would validate
> our simple self-defense.*

My heritage has lasted longer than any other in the world. Its survival has been based on the fact that it has been and is industrious, beautiful, intelligent, and dignified. No matter how hard or how often the attempt is made to convince me otherwise, I will live and die knowing and celebrating the depth, wonder, and power of the African Spirit living in and through all of us who share it. We are the hope of the future! We are the children of God!

℘

The youth I couldn't seem to do anything for was my son, Eli. When he was thirteen, I panicked and tricked him into an adolescent drug treatment program. He wasn't using drugs rampantly as yet, but he was suffering and I didn't know what to do. His father had been a raging alcoholic and in a facility for juvenile delinquents by the time he was eleven. In fact, after five years of marriage, he and I had split up over his drinking and the last I heard, he was drinking yet. So, when I saw Eli starting to hit the streets, I moved with dispatch in what turned out to be a futile attempt to save him.

Eli never had an opportunity to grow up as an ordinary White boy. He was exposed to Black culture from a young age and had learned to recognize institutional oppression against people of color even as he was learning how to read or hit a baseball. At one point, he told me that I had made him so "political" that sometimes, he didn't have anyone his age to talk to, particularly in Tallahassee.

"I know," I acknowledged sadly. "Sometimes I feel the same way, but when I get lonely, I ask myself if I would really *want* to think like all the rest of them...and I decide I wouldn't. Would you?"

He agreed that he wouldn't either, but it is not the same to be thirteen as it is to be grown. And he was thirteen and White in Tallahassee, Florida. I cannot imagine what his pain must have been or what better path I might have tried to help him find. Eventually, nearly a decade later, he would be diagnosed with bi-polar disorder, though I never understood how they could make a decent determination since he was generally either high or coming down.

When he left the program a couple of years later, we were invited across the street to a birthday celebration at a Black neighbor's house. We didn't know the family well, but had included their children in our July 4th festivities and they had not forgotten. The weather was great on the day of the barbeque. The food was good. The adults were sipping beer. And Eli, at fifteen, wound up at a card table in the yard playing spades with several Black men in their early twenties.

I knew it would be bad form to act or even be nervous about it, but he was *winning*, slapping the cards on the table and talking "smack" just like they were, and the drunker the other players got, the more I just wanted to extricate him and go home. At some point, I got the opportunity to follow him back to our house long enough to ask him if he was sure he knew what he was doing.

"You know they're getting drunk, Eli. I mean, you're a kid and they're losing. Aren't you concerned that there's gonna be some kind of trouble?"

"Look, Mom," he explained, just short of sounding pained, as he sometimes did in trying to remind me that he had shot craps when he was seven and had been around Black folks all his life. "I'm not trying to be Black. See what I'm wearing? I'm wearing a Metallica t-shirt and Jenko jeans. If I was trying to pretend to be something I'm not, they might feel they need to teach me a lesson. But I know how to respect myself and respect them. There's not gonna be any trouble."

And there wasn't. Years later, after he and his girlfriend had brought their cats and followed me to Ft. Lauderdale, he told me that he had eventually become a member of a Black street gang in Tallahassee and that the only problem he ever had in doing so was that they had kept pressing him to cut his waist-length hair, which he would not do.

Inner cities a war zone says scholar

NEWS EDITOR

Rebecca Hensley describes the daily war in America's inner cities, with police officers on one side of the battle line and African-American men on the other.

It's not a declared war, the Florida State University doctoral student says, but both camps know they're in it.

"There's no confusion, and that's what's so scary," Hensley said Monday.

Hensley will talk tonight at the Center for Professional Development about the ongoing "war" in America's inner cities. Her lecture is sponsored by the FSU Center for African-American Culture.

A sociology student specializing in race relations and urban issues, Hensley has been studying the interaction between police officers and African-American men off and on for the last 20 years. She predicted the L.A. race riots last summer, and she anticipated the Worthington Park disturbances in Tallahassee last fall.

"Every time things like this happen we put our hands on our cheek and say 'oh my, how'd this happen,' as if we didn't set it up in the first place," Hensley said Monday.

She argues that unless white America begins to seriously address the institutionalized oppression of African-Americans, violent disturbances will continue to erupt.

"We keep saying we're doing the best we can, but in the meantime we have people who have been waiting for 400 years, some of whom have gone crazy. ... If we saw the same scenario in another society, we'd expect people to rise up," Hensley said.

"For African-Americans as a whole, things have not changed much in the last 25 years, and on a daily basis, many people's lives have gotten worse," she added. "Then we wonder why they're frustrated."

Hensley believes that police officers are used by society to maintain an illusion of law and order in inner cities where larger social problems such as poverty and unemployment exist.

"We push law enforcement officers out in front of us and say 'make them be quiet,' " Hensley said. "It's like sprinkling pixie dust and saying take two pills and you'll be fine in the morning. It doesn't work like that. It's going to get worse and I don't want that to happen."

Hensley developed many of her ideas two years ago when she ran into two sheriff's deputies from another county in a laundromat. The deputies described their mission as a battle for control in which police use such methods as "slam dunking" men's heads into the hoods of cars to show that they have control over the inner-city community.

Hensley subsequently interviewed two unemployed African-American men who described similar methods used by police in their neighborhoods.

The result, Hensley said, is a raging war with no winners.

"Both sides are put in a trick bag by the rest of society, which doesn't seem to be interested in addressing the issues of institutionalized racism," she said. "The whole situation sets up an opportunity for madness on both sides."

Hensley said she sees herself as a lighthouse, warning people that more violence will ensue unless they begin to push for social change.

"We've got a hole in the bottom of the boat and we need to understand we're all in it together," she said. "History, logic, common sense and sociology are all separate, but they would all suggest that social problems unaddressed exacerbate and come home to roost. The sad thing is, when the chickens come home to roost, people act surprised ... when we had time all along to do something about it."

Hensley will speak tonight at 7 in room 123A at the Center for Professional Development.

Front Page, Florida Flambeau 3/31/93

1992

One afternoon, while I was at a laundromat washing clothes, I met a couple of White Sheriff's deputies from a county located in another part of the state. They were in Tallahassee to take some specialized training and were doing their laundry, as well, so we struck up a conversation. I told them that I was a sociologist at FSU with a specialization in race relations and then started asking them questions about policing in the inner city. Their answers so alarmed me that I asked them if it was okay for me to take notes. Not only did they agree to this, but they gave me their phone numbers at work in their home county with an invitation to "ride along" anytime I could come for a visit.

From what they said, they were admitting that it was not at all uncommon for them to "shake-down" dealers for dope (which they destroyed) and money (which they kept) and then set them free. Moreover, they described a routine practice they called "slam-dunking," wherein they bashed a Black man's head into the hood of a car, throwing blood everywhere, to "send a message."

"You have to talk to them in a language they understand," one of the deputies said. "You *have* to have those people's respect. Otherwise, they'll beat *you* up. And you won't be able to get anything you're supposed to get out of that community."

"In training," the other deputy chimed in, "they tell you all this stuff about how to talk to people in a professional manner. Then, the first time you're standing out in front of a bar in the middle of the night and you say to some Black guy, 'All right, sir, I'm going to have to arrest you pursuant to Florida statute blah-blah-blah...,' he turns around and punches you flat in the face. Right then is when you realize that *this* is the *real* world and they never told you *anything* in training about what to do next."

"So you get beaten up in front of 250 people," the first one jumped back in, "and you're humiliated. Next time, you're gonna make damn sure that doesn't happen to you again. Otherwise, you won't be able to come into that community at all. They won't pay any attention to you unless you meet them on their terms."

I was trying not to gasp. I was writing down everything and they were just talking as casually as if they were describing the weather.

"You can't talk the same way to a person who has a Master's degree and a person with a second grade education," explained the first deputy further. "We have to be able to do both. Our survival depends on it. So we learn how to grab 'em, slam dunk 'em on the car, cuff 'em, stuff 'em, and get the hell out of there when that's the way they want it."

"It's been suggested," I queried, trying not to sound *too* "liberal," "that young African-American men have had their personhood so assaulted by this society that they perceive their only hope of psychological survival to be in coming against 'the system' in any way they can — even using crime as a guerrilla struggle of sorts. Do you think this is true?"

Neither deputy agreed with this statement at all.

"Blacks have the same opportunities as everybody else," said one flatly. "They just don't *want* to do any better...for some reason...otherwise they would."

"You know," added the other. "We have conversations like this all the time between ourselves, but we don't usually talk to anybody else about it. We'll sit around the room trying to figure it all out and finally we'll say, 'what the hell, let's go get a beer.'"

I was dumbfounded.

Within a week, I had located and interviewed several African-American men who had had dealings with the Tallahassee police.

Asked if they thought the police were racist in nature, one of them replied, "They're just trying to get us to show them some respect."

Then he went on. "The young ones just be out there selling drugs and stuff right in the cops' faces — doing anything they want right in full view, not showing any respect at all. And the cops don't like it. But what they don't understand is: they have to *give* respect to *get* it. The cops have more people on the street than the dealers do."

"What do you mean by that?" I asked.

"Well," he continued, "they arrest somebody for selling drugs, but they don't take him downtown. They just take some money from him and put him back out there to make some more. That stuff goes on steady — all the time."

"And are African-American law enforcement officers different from White ones?" I asked further.

"You have to remember," one of the other men interrupted, "that these guys have to keep their jobs. That officer may be Black, but his supervisor will be White, so that

Black policeman has to keep everybody in the department convinced all the time that he's on their side or he'll be gone."

When I questioned the men about whether law enforcement personnel used violence in the inner city in Tallahassee, they blurted "Oh, *yeah*!" in unison.

"They'll hand-cuff a guy," continued one of the men, "and slam him into the hood of a car in front of everybody to make sure everybody knows that that can happen to them, too. They're trying to send a message to everybody watching. And that's the way they try to control us."

"And how do folks feel about that?" I asked.

"Well," replied another one of the men I was interviewing, "you know all those White people that've been gettin' beat up for no good reason — just somebody runs up and starts hittin' 'em? Well, that's Black men sending a message back to the police. It's all about control. And if they don't stop what they're doing, up the road, it's gonna get worse. We already beat 'em up when we get 'em alone."

"But you never see that in the paper," I protested.

"They aren't gonna print that," one of the men responded. "They'd be too ashamed."

1993

When Jeanette came up pregnant, we were all excited, but I was a little concerned. Jeanette was in her mid-twenties, and received a check from the government for being "handicapped," she said. She didn't like it and had wanted to work instead, but they wouldn't give her a chance to learn a trade. She was angry and hurt and I agreed with her. The woman I had come to know was fully capable of holding a job and would have been able to make considerably more than she was getting on Supplementary Security Income or whatever it was. She had resigned herself to sitting in the swing or watching television shows all day, but she clearly felt disappointed with her life. Still, I wondered if she was really ready to be a mother.

As she approached full term, Mervin asked me if I would be willing to come get them and take them to the hospital when the time came. They must have known other people with cars, or Medicaid might even have paid for an ambulance, but for whatever reason, he asked me and, though I was about to begin my final exams that semester, I said yes.

"I may have to just take you and drop you off, though," I warned them. And Mervin assured me that this would be fine.

Several days later, the phone rang at about 1:30 a.m. the night before one of my exams. I was studying, but felt there was no choice. Sighing, exhausted and wondering why in the world I had committed to this, I put on my shoes and jumped in the car.

By the time we arrived at the hospital twenty minutes later, I knew that Jeanette was in no shape emotionally to handle this thing on her own. She was so terrified she couldn't speak. I dropped them at the Emergency Room entrance and went to park the car. Apparently, she was pretty well dilated because, when I went upstairs after parking, I found Mervin and Jeanette already in a delivery room surrounded by medical personnel.

Unfortunately, however, Jeanette's muscles were stiff with panic and had clamped down in such a way that the poor baby couldn't come down the vaginal canal to be born. So minutes turned into an hour while the frustrated, though sympathetic, doctors and nurses tried to figure out what to do short of a C-section.

I talked and talked and *talked* to Jeanette, trying everything to get her to relax until finally, somehow, a doctor was able to get hold of the baby — a girl — and pull her to freedom. We all exclaimed with relief as the umbilical cord was cut and Mervin and Jeanette's new daughter was cleaned up and put in her mother's arms.

"*So,*" I said jovially, looking at the smiling mother and her new off-spring, "What are you going to call your little girl?"

Mervin and Jeanette looked up at once.

"Morgan," they replied together.

Tears welled up in my eyes.

"Well," I said, when I could pull myself together, "I guess I better go home and finish studying for my exam."

As I left the delivery room, I turned in the doorway and thanked everybody for their hard work.

"Thank **you**!" they all responded in one voice, smiling.

* * *

It was probably about a year later when I was driving down a street late one afternoon and saw Mervin walking along on the sidewalk. When he told me that he was headed for home, I offered him a ride, which he accepted.

I was feeling very dejected. My son Eli, at sixteen, was now smoking crack and shooting heroin. His life was out of control and, since he still slept at my house much of the time, to some extent my life was, too. Morgan won a "Just Say No" contest at her middle school with a poster that read, "Don't Do Drugs — It Will Tear Your Family Apart." In addition, after nearly five years single, I had tried getting married again in 1991, but this time, after only two years, my husband had hung himself, leaving me an emotionally exhausted and financially overwhelmed widow.

Added to my personal devastation, then, was the pressure created by the fact that, besides teaching three classes to support myself and my family, I was trying to work on my dissertation entitled "On Rationalizing Racism: Institutionalized Oppression in Sociological Writings on African-American/European-American Relations." Despite all the emotional upheaval in my life, I had four articles on "revise and re-submit" status to various scientific journals, I had just won the department's Graduate Student Teacher of the Year award, and I had been cited as one of the fifteen best graduate student teachers on the whole campus.

While I was accomplishing all that, I had also somehow managed to finish my Ph.D. coursework, successfully clear three comprehensive examinations, and have the first four chapters of my dissertation accepted by my committee. I was officially a Ph.D. candidate now, instead of just a student, but I had nothing left emotionally and didn't feel able to go on.

"You *have* to go on," Melvin urged without apology. "Jeanette and I can't go to school and get a Ph.D. We can't tell our story ourselves. Who will tell our story, if **you** don't?"

I tried to cling to his words like a life preserver in an ocean of pain, but several months later, when the Sociology Department chair at FSU told me that my funding was being pulled just before the graduate student advisor called me in to suggest that maybe I should just get out of higher education, I buckled. Offered a tenure-track position at the University of Northern Alabama, I turned it down because Morgan and I didn't belong in northern Alabama. And leaving Eli behind because he said he didn't want to go, Morgan and I left for south Florida.

Being in Tallahassee had taken a terrible toll on Morgan. To begin with, few of the White children at school would have anything much to do with her because she was Black. At the same time, the Black children rejected her because she was light-skinned, beautiful, and had waist-length hair that hung in big loose curls. After reading Toni Morrison's The Bluest Eye, I decided that they might be jealous of her "good" hair, so I cut it short in hopes that it would help. It didn't.

Eventually, Morgan settled on two best friends: one Korean and one from Brazil. They were sweet girls and good students, but they couldn't save Morgan from Tallahassee. Only a year after we arrived, when asked by some African-American students how she thought of herself, Morgan replied not with a proud "Black *and* White," the way she had in Macomb, but rather, looking at the floor, a mumbled, "mixed."

I was deeply disheartened. I hadn't noticed that happening and I didn't think that our perspective as a family had changed from what it had always been. At one point, for example, I had taken Eli and Morgan to a counter-demonstration being held to protest the Ku Klux Klan's appearance in robes and hoods right in the middle of downtown. We returned home afterward with a small strip of white cloth that had been "liberated" by an El Salvadoran friend of ours who had grabbed the hood right off one Klansman's head and torn it into little pieces that he passed into the crowd while the outraged man looked on, sputtering.

I had also inadvertently appeared on the local television news on a different occasion for being caught on camera yelling nose-to-nose at a Klansman in a park. We maintained our on-going friendship with Mervin and Jeanette and Morgan's namesake. And for a while, Morgan and I even attended a large African-American church where I sang in the choir. But in spite of our continuing family activities, Morgan had become "mixed" and the wound went so deep that it took her years to recover.

She wouldn't discuss it. Whenever I would raise the issue of her racial category, she would absolutely refuse to get involved in the conversation. I was reminded again of what the young woman had yelled at me at the Black family conference. But I now knew that when she only focused on my inability as a White woman to raise a Black child, she had chosen not to mention another crucial aspect of our situation. The fact is that in reality, Morgan might be Black by the operating historical and cultural standards in the United States, but in Tallahassee, I came to understand that she wasn't going to be immediately accepted by her own community without a trial. Morgan would have to be her own chief witness. And I, as a White woman, would only be allowed to sit in the back row and watch.

Still, I was determined that, if my life was to be shattered anyway, at least I needed to give her a chance to live somewhere she could see other people that looked like her, go to school with African-American children that didn't reject her out of hand, and find her Blackness.

PART FIVE

1994

Morgan and I arrived in Ft. Lauderdale on a Friday night in August with just enough money for a security deposit and one month's rent on a little two-bedroom apartment. By this time, we were used to living in houses, however less than fancy, and we felt as if we were living in a cave, not to mention tightly surrounded on every side and overhead by people we didn't know. It was months before I could afford to have the television cable hooked up, which meant that our primary entertainment became watching the ducks walk around, pecking and pooping on the concrete slab the complex called our patio. We missed Eli. We missed our friends. And we were so bored that one night I came in from work and found Morgan reduced to watching a football game announced in Spanish on one of the two snowy channels we managed somehow to receive.

There were a lot of Latino families in the other apartments where we lived and more than a few Puerto Ricans. Soon, Morgan was wearing big gold hoops in her ears and pulling the sides of her long, dark hair up into a top knot, leaving the rest hanging loose down her back.

"Are you trying to look Puerto Rican?" I challenged her playfully one night, especially since she could easily pass for that ethnicity.

"No," she replied, looking a little defensive.

But the hoops and the top knot shortly disappeared. She was, as a Buddhist would call it, "choosing and playing with options." I should have just trusted the process. It was out of my control in any case.

Frantic to get a job, any job, anywhere, and as quickly as possible, I applied for and took a position working with juvenile delinquents in a brand new residential program about to open in North Miami. Since I had just spent seven years in graduate school, going from campus to campus like an intellectual gypsy, I felt lucky to have found a job at all. I hadn't, after all, ever demonstrated a commitment to any particular employment track. Except for graduate school, which I had finally left without finishing at the Ph.D. level, I had rarely stayed more than a year in any job. I had spent five years as a homemaker and another five years on welfare in my thirties. And, at forty-eight years of age, as an oddly and over-qualified job-seeker with a very patchy record of employment, I was competing with highly-focused young Master's degree-holding college graduates who knew where they were headed and had already distinguished themselves by their stability.

Fortunately for me, the state of Florida had just created a Department of Juvenile Justice to deal more effectively, they hoped, with youth who broke the law. The determination that this was needed came directly out of an incident that occurred near Tallahassee while we were living there, when a German tourist at a rest stop was shot to death in the process of a robbery. The robbery was ultimately blamed on an

African-American teenager, though there were many, many questions that were never answered about the situation, largely because the need for an immediate resolution was at a hyper-pitch. The legislators meeting barely thirty miles away, out of respect for the tourist industry in one of the premier vacation spots of the world, and in response to bellowing from multiple interests, found a huge amount of money to establish one of only a few such departments in the nation. Residential and day programs popped up across the state on October 1, 1994, like mushrooms in a forest after a heavy rain, and one of these programs hired me to develop and implement its "employment readiness" segment.

The overall program sort of designed itself as it went along. I think maybe the agency administrators thought the person they hired to direct the program would just know what to do. Unfortunately for all of us, this turned out not to be true. In fact, several weeks after the first cadre of "residents" were ensconced, there was a mini-uprising on a Saturday afternoon. "The Boyz," as I came to refer to them, just took over the place — unexpectedly, needless to say. One minute we were planning groups for later in the day and the next minute, there were thirteen- to seventeen-year-old males — almost every one of which was African-American, Jamaican, or Haitian — bouncing off the walls and taking the staff with them.

Interestingly enough, I had been walking around for the several days just previous to this feeling sorry for myself.

"How did I wind up here?" I would think or even mumble to myself — sometimes teary-eyed — as I walked from building to building at the facility where the program was housed. "I just spent seven years in grad school. I'm supposed to be standing in front of a college classroom, not riding herd on a passel of children who can't even sit still. These are *animals*, not *humans*!"

As if I had called them out to show off, they went just crazy enough the next Saturday to really introduce themselves. I was terrified. I wasn't particularly afraid that they were going to hurt me, for some reason, although I was keenly aware all of a sudden that I was wearing expensive glasses that I couldn't begin to replace on the salary I was being paid. But I was deathly afraid that they were going to do harm to one another and that we wouldn't be able to prevent it. After all, that was ostensibly how it had all started: some kind of altercation between two of the boys.

At what was very nearly my breaking point, one of the men who had been working with this population for years got right in my face, eyeball to eyeball, and said in a low voice, but with great firmness, "Don't...you...***dare***! You're the only woman in here right now and they're watching you like a *hawk*." Eventually, I learned that what he was getting at was that if I buckled under the pressure, the kids would never respect me or listen to me again. They would force me to leave the job with my tail between my legs and I *needed* this job. So, though I didn't yet really get his meaning, I snapped out of my panic and found my sense of humor somewhere in the mix.

A few minutes later, I shut one kid in an office (accompanied by another staff member to protect the computers). With my sneaker pressed against the base of the door, I was pulling on the doorknob so that the youth could not burst out of the room. My other hand was spread out solidly in the middle of another kid's chest, keeping him away from the door.

"Well," I quipped to a staff member corralling a third boy on the other side of the room, "I guess this means we won't be having group..."

When we called the program manager, he told us not to call the police and not to leave. He, of course, never showed up. Four hours and a few holes in the walls later, the boys got tired of the game and decided to eat dinner. On my way home, it occurred to me in a blinding flash of the obvious that there had not been a single drop of blood shed all afternoon. It was apparent that they had been in control. If they had wanted to do more than break a couple of light fixtures, they could have. I decided that they were just bored and living up to their reputations, but that I certainly would never be afraid of them again. Respectful of what they were capable of, yes; afraid of what they might do to me or even to each other, not much.

I started out planning the groups I would run using ideas that were based on common sense more than anything else, bolstered by research I had done when studying youth gang members in Tallahassee. The purpose of my position was to increase their employability, so I had a wide range of possible directions in which to move, or at least I thought I did until I held the first group.

We were in an upstairs room and there were probably about a dozen boys. I had a handout with slots for them to write in answers to simple, but direct questions. It rapidly became apparent that more than half of them couldn't read the sheet at a functional level and that fewer than that could spell or write their answers in the spaces provided. I was nonplussed, but trying to make the necessary adjustments to my game plan without losing their interest or having them feel embarrassed by their lack of skills. It hardly mattered. They weren't ready to listen anyway.

They wouldn't stay in their seats. One of them was looking out the window. Another was pounding out a drumbeat on a bookshelf with his hands. One leaped up to do an impromptu series of very adept dance moves for several minutes without interruption. And yet another was, I swear, peeling off the strips that covered the joints in the newly painted dry wall. I quickly went from nonplussed to incredulous. How was I going to be of any use to these boys at all, I wondered?

Getting to know them as individuals gave me the answer to my question. They were as widely variegated as any group of individuals could possibly have been. But their commonalities were heart-rending. They often had mentally ill, addicted, uncaring, or incapable parents. They often exhibited the characteristics of having been badly abused or molested. They supported whole families by selling drugs or stealing cars. And they had already learned that, as it is often said in prison, "a man's gotta do what a man's gotta do."

"Where are the White kids?" I asked one of the other workers, puzzled.

"In psych programs, mostly," I was told. "Or private schools. Or programs for adolescent addicts. Or even out-patient programs."

"Where they get treatment instead of punishment," I added in my mind.

Eventually, I learned about the way Black kids, and particularly Black boys, are singled out at the age of ten or even younger wherever they are seen in public by the police. Even that young, they are rousted (asked what they are doing, where they live, and who they are) in ways that White children would never be. In many cities, they will be stopped on a street or in a park and have their photos taken right there with numbers across their chests so that files can be built long before they ever break a law, a bitter prediction that such a day will come. Sociologists have long told us that this type of practice is "criminogenic." It actually produces crime. It says to children: "You are a criminal," and, if they accept that "master status" as their own, they will, in fact, believe it and become it, as if in perfect harmony with the socialization crafted especially for them.

In Florida, there is even a law just for Black boys. It's called "prowling," and means that they have been found in a neighborhood where they don't "belong." White youth who might be arrested for loitering — or might not — are virtually never arrested for "prowling," which brings with it a different level of concern and a different set of consequences. At least this is what I was told by various members of law enforcement groups at the time.

When you add all this to the way that internalized and institutionalized oppression has taken its toll and impressed itself in myriad ways throughout their community and their families, these children's involvement with law enforcers amounts to a foregone conclusion. A conclusion many of them grow up expecting. All of the boys in our program knew men and were related to men who had been or were in prison. Current statistics now warn that at the present rate, a third of the Black boys born in 2001 can expect to go to prison, while three-fourths of those presently incarcerated are there for non-violent crimes (such as possession of a crack pipe stem) or no crime at all (such as appearing for a probation appointment on the wrong day). When you consider that it costs as much as $40,000 per year to keep a man in prison and even more to lock up a juvenile, you realize how badly our society wants to make sure that millions of Black men are out of circulation and doomed to a lifetime of addiction, ill health (both physically and mentally), and joblessness. Eventually, I started telling the boys that the most revolutionary act they could commit would be to learn to read.

When I asked one very poised and articulate fourteen-year-old whether he had ever earned any money legally, he reminded me indignantly, "I'm too *young* to have a job!" Ultimately, I discovered that, due to his intelligence and the necessity of trying to help his single mother support his seven younger siblings at home, Antonio had developed a very savvy level of business acumen. He could do math in his head faster than I could and dispassionately discussed the process of "parlaying" a small amount of drugs into the rent or school shoes for everybody with the finesse of a corporate CEO.

About a year later, after I had been tapped by the Department of Juvenile Justice to help train their workers in south Florida, I was standing in front of the staff of a program in Miami, talking about "What To Do When Your Buttons Get Pushed" or some such topic, when I looked out a picture window just in time to see a police car pull over across the street. Two officers got out of the car and accosted a Black adolescent walking along the sidewalk with another boy. School had just let out and there were a number of young people up and down the street, but the police went straight for this kid.

Even at a distance, it was apparent that the White officer was asking the youth a question. Whatever it was he answered in reply, the officer reached out all of a sudden and, using the heel of his hand, smacked the boy in the middle of his forehead hard enough to bounce the back of the kid's head against the brick wall just behind him. There was a pause. Another question. Another response. Another smack into the wall. The youth stood with his arms down, receiving the blows like he knew better than to fight back. And other people were just walking past the drama as if they didn't see it.

"Excuse me," I said abruptly, interrupting my training session. "I'll be right back." And with that, I walked out the front door and, avoiding the traffic, strode purposefully across the street.

I had barely left the sidewalk when I realized that the youth being struck repeatedly was Antonio. I approached the scene without hesitation. "Are you all right, Ant?" I asked him, receiving a small nod before turning in time to hear the police officer instruct me to step away.

"Who are you?" the officer demanded to know, frowning.

"I'm with the Department of Juvenile Justice," I replied evenly in a conciliatory tone, holding his eyes with my own. "I've been watching what's been going on from across the street..."

"Well, you don't need to be here, so move along," he commanded.

"I have a legal right to be here," I countered, knowing how crucial witnesses can be in situations like this. "I've worked with this boy and I'd be happy to be of service..."

Before I could say anything else, the officer simply ordered Antonio into the back of the squad car and drove off. Making calls later, I found that no arrests had been made that afternoon in that neighborhood and that no one carrying Antonio's name had been arrested at all. I exulted, choosing to believe that they had felt forced to release the boy around the corner rather than to have to worry about whether or not I was going to report them for hitting him without justification. But in retrospect, I look back and remember the frozen look on Antonio's face as he headed for the car, not looking at me, while I kept repeating over and over, as if repeating it would make it true, "It's gonna be alright, Antonio...It's gonna be alright." Was it fear on his face or rage or hopelessness, a combination of them all, or what? The fact is I'll never know.

That's the way it usually is for White people that have even a tiny clue: we can be witnesses, but when push comes to shove, it's seldom the back of *our* heads being smacked into the brick wall. It's seldom *us* in the police car unjustly. And African-Americans know this too well. They may appreciate having a witness. They are deadly aware that something that simple can sometimes save their lives. But they have to resent it, as well. Why do *their* lives require witnesses to keep them from being lied about, man-handled, or even murdered?

Actually, murder is not always the worst thing that can happen to a young Black man in the United States. Sometimes it's his spirit that is lynched, leaving his body to dangle kicking just above the ground for the rest of his life for all the world to see...and learn from.

When I first met Maxwell at the facility, his shy smile and quiet ways captured me almost immediately, despite the "grill" of gold he sported ostentatiously across the front of his upper teeth. His hair was in short "dreads," little tufts of twisted hair that he turned and pulled almost constantly, as if to comfort and distract himself from his circumstances.

At one of our first private sessions, intended to help me evaluate his principle issues and needs related to "employability," it was established that Maxwell, typical of youth who get into trouble with the law, was not usually connecting his behavior with its consequences. In all fairness to Maxwell and all of the other Black girls and boys just like him, negative behavior on their parts is not always necessary to get them awful results. In fact, I discovered eventually that Maxwell had been literally beaten within an inch of his life by mistake. A police officer who thought Maxwell was someone else had beaten him mercilessly with a nightstick on a public street corner in broad daylight one afternoon when he was fourteen-years-old, causing so much damage to his skull that he still slurred his words slightly. Maxwell's mother, who was from Jamaica, had not understood that she could sue for medical and even punitive damages on behalf of her terribly injured son, so Maxwell didn't even get all the subsequent medical care that he needed. The police department involved paid his immediate hospital bills and dropped the charges, acknowledging their mistake, and that was the sum total of their acceptance of responsibility in the matter.

Still, Maxwell, either because his critical thinking skills were lacking or because of the injury to his brain, was not computing the ways in which he was affecting his own life. When I saw the boys one-on-one, I often gave them what I called a "prescription," an index card on which I had written a reminder of something specific they needed to think about or practice until our next session. Maxwell's prescription said simply, "What I do determines what happens to me."

Several days later, in the courtyard of the program facility, Maxwell jumped in to help a friend who was being roughed up by the police and he was taken to the Detention Center downtown during the evening hours when I wasn't present. A month later, when he finally returned, he told me that the entire time he had been in detention, he had kept his "prescription" tucked into the metal springs of the bunk above where he slept. He showed me that it was still in his pocket. And that afternoon at dinner time, he sat beside me where I was monitoring the dining room and, looking straight ahead, not at me, he said quietly, "I wonder what it would be like to be a regular person."

From that day forward, even after I moved on to the Department of Juvenile Justice, even after he graduated from the program, I tried to work with Maxwell. I met his mother. I maintained an interest in how and what he was doing, and I spoke with him or saw him on a semi-regular basis. He definitely knew that I cared about him and believed in him.

But Maxwell's mother did not understand the situation he had fallen into by coming to the attention of the local law enforcement representatives. At one pivotal moment when he was no longer under supervision, I pled with her to sign the necessary forms so that Maxwell could go for training at a Job Corps facility in another city. He was nearly seventeen-years-old and wanted to acquire a trade. But she couldn't bring herself to let go of her youngest child and so the moment passed.

I remember the last time I saw him before he got locked up again. We had gone to a music festival where we ate and drank ginger sodas and Maxwell bought me a cowl shell bracelet which he made me promise always to keep to remind me that he would always be grateful for my being his friend.

On the way home, I tried to warn him that he could not leave his mother's house after dark any more without exciting the police who I tried to describe humorously as "Marauding Monsters" who wanted to eat him up. He laughed and said he understood, but he was young and bored and he kept going out. When he was arrested for being involved in a burglary the following year, the dominos fell hard and fast. It was three years before he would be released from prison, and then only to be deported to a country he had not seen since he was six and where he had no family support.

A few months after he had first gone to the adult county jail, Maxwell called me and said succinctly in his soft, slurred voice, "Something happened to me in here and I know that now my life will never be the same." And I'm sure he was right.

There is no doubt that Maxwell committed the burglary that finally put him into the jail, but I am a sociologist. I believe that, if we really want to know what caused something, we need to go all the way back in the causal chain and not just stop at what came immediately before it. Things might have been different for Maxwell if he hadn't been beaten that time, if the authorities had given his mother the information and financial assistance she should have gotten after the beating, if he'd gotten the medical and psychological help he needed when it was most crucial, if his mother had not been afraid to let him go to the Job Corps facility when I suggested it, if young Black men with dreadlocks didn't draw police like honey draws flies. As the young men have learned so painfully to say, "It's all good." But it's not.

As long as we have enough money to lock up troubled kids of color, but not enough money to fund summer work programs at less than a tenth of the cost, it won't be good. As long as we continue to pretend that the soul-grinding effects of life-long abject poverty are somehow the fault of the Black community instead of the fault of White decision-makers at every corporate and governmental level across our nation, it won't be good. And as long as we let one child be blamed and brutalized for being born into a world not of their making, it won't be good for any of us, whatever lies we tell ourselves.

1997

By the fall of 1997, I had been hired by the Florida Department of Juvenile Justice to work in its Ft. Lauderdale office as staff to the Juvenile Justice Board in Broward County. The Juvenile Justice Board was made up of movers and shakers from offices and agencies throughout the county. Representatives from city and county government, the school board, the social service community, the business community, the courts, and law enforcement met monthly to discuss how issues related to juvenile law-breaking could best be approached locally. The Board served as the liaison to the Florida DJJ, in constant communication with Tallahassee, and individual members arm-wrestled issues in and outside of the meetings in a most impressive fashion from where I stood as a newcomer to this arena.

As is virtually always the case in such matters, the most profound focus of individual and Board interest had to do with the funding that was flowing pretty freely at the time from the state level. Besides the multi-millions being spent annually by the Department itself in every possible locale — including Broward County — to adjudicate and supervise youth, there were additional millions to be accessed and spent locally, a process that the Board members not only oversaw, but benefited from professionally and sometimes even personally. Grant proposals would be received, reviewed, and evaluated, with award depending primarily on the recommendations of the Board, some of whose members represented the agencies applying for the funds. There were long-time power players at the table and the power struggle *du jour* could reach epic proportions over what might not always be issues of monumental importance. It was a major opportunity for me and I was prepared to make the most of it.

I had always been good at "working a room," my euphemism for the consciously crafted practice of walking into a room full of people and going from person to person, touching base, feeling out, broaching subjects, making connections. When I was sixteen, for example, I went to Girls' State in Illinois. Nominated and supported by American Legion Auxiliaries from across the state, I and 499 other teen-aged girls representing 500 different high schools descended on a small college campus and were guided through a rapid-fire reproduction of the state political process. Its purpose, of course, is to introduce young women who are identified as demonstrating leadership characteristics to the world of politics in the interest of encouraging them to stay involved.

The furious pace of the Girls' State experience was a little overwhelming, but when the dust settled, I had managed to be elected Secretary of State by the highest margin of votes they could ever remember up to that time. I had received nearly 400 of the 500 votes possible — after "campaigning" for only three days. One reason this occurred was that I had the unconditional support of a girl I had just met who committed herself absolutely to seeing me win. Another factor involved was that an impromptu speech I had to give before the entire assembly on only ten minutes notice brought down the house. But it was also true that I sat at a different table in the dining room at every meal, introducing and ingratiating myself like a veteran of the art. As a matter of fact, many of the men in my mother's family have been lawyers at least as far back as 1800, with a number of them running for and being elected to office, including to the Governorship of Kentucky. So maybe it's in the genes.

Anyway, I quickly found my niche among the players at the Juvenile Justice Board table, being helpful, remembering my place, learning who was who and what was what, thanks largely to the out-going Board Coordinator's coffee-driven conversations. In short order, I was able to find ways to put my own agendas forward, as well, most of which revolved in one way or another around the socially-constructed political notion of race. In spite of the fact that well over half of the boys and girls adjudicated to the Department of Juvenile Justice were Black and in certain categories, 70% to 90% were Black, only two of the eighteen or twenty members of Broward County's Juvenile Justice Board at the time were African-American. Fortunately, they were up to the task, though I watched it try them sorely on many occasions.

There was a whole string of Board committees that met between its monthly meetings, but my hands-down favorite was the Cultural Competence Committee, where I found intelligent, capable individuals who were as committed as I was to educating the community at all levels about the institutionalized oppression of Black people. Millions of dollars were being spent by the Department of Juvenile Justice and other funding sources on residential and non-residential programs that were often full of Black youth, but workers and administrators in these programs remained by and large in some sort of colossal state of denial about the effects of covert, overt, and internalized racism on these children's daily lives.

The meetings of the Cultural Competence Committee were intense, focused, and often reflective of the kind of humor that characterizes gatherings of people who already understand each other's perspectives and are unified in their concerns. The CCC meetings offered an opportunity, among other things, to express what often could not be easily expressed at meetings of the entire Board without creating great turbulence or, at least, discomfort. They also served as a forum to create a curriculum that would raise the consciousness, first of the Board itself, and then of decision-makers throughout the county. I was grateful for the opportunity to be a part of this team and often felt, as I suspect the others must have, that without these sessions, watching the workings of the greater Board, knowing what Black youth were facing every day, would be too painful to bear.

As I recall, it was at one of these Cultural Competence Committee meetings that I first came to be scrutinized more closely by a program director named Randi. Randi, who dressed like a power-player, was a take-charge White woman and ran a large, long-standing Broward County social service agency that provided services to many at-risk youth and their families. There was an immense amount of funding pouring through the agency — much more than many others received — and its statistics documented a serious skewing of their services toward White youth. Scuttle-butt had it that most of the workers at Randi's agency were not prepared to work with children of color and did not do it well, so Black children and their families typically did not return for scheduled appointments and the agency could then legitimately report them as having refused to participate, rather than as agency failures. Unfortunately, this often meant that the youth in question might be "bumped up" to a more intense involvement with the Department of Juvenile Justice, in spite of the fact that the problem didn't belong to the youth.

In any case, Randi was an odd addition to the Cultural Competence Committee and only attended, as I recall, a couple of the meetings before dropping out again. I didn't have much personal contact with her after that until we began seeing each other at Truancy Task Force meetings.

The Truancy Task Force had been established originally as a committee of the Juvenile Justice Board, but over a period of about a year's time, it definitely took on a life of its own. For one thing, it was an idea whose time had come. Similar groups had developed not only all over Florida, but all over the country more or less simultaneously in an attempt to address a problem that had reached what was finally admitted to be epidemic proportions. Additionally, the Broward Sheriff's Office was backing it heavily with space, personnel, and both technological and financial assistance.

The bottom line was that, on any given day at that time, more than 10,000 students in Broward County were not showing up for school where they were legally mandated to be. Middle school youth, in particular, were tuning out the educational establishment and turning, instead, to boredom, drugs, gangs, and crime. Sheriff's deputies would conduct a mid-morning sweep on occasion and pull as many as a hundred or more kids off the streets in one loop. But as the Truancy Task Force escalated in its determination and effort to keep kids in school, it became apparent eventually that the old stick-and-carrot routine wasn't going to do the job. Yes, you could arrest them for not being in school. And yes, you could even arrest or fine parents when their children were not in school. And yes, you could implement programming to intrigue youth more or bring them up to speed with their skills. But the problem of what we came to call "root causes" would not be denied. The problem was bigger than one child making one decision on one particular day.

Truancy Task Force meetings could wrangle their way through subjects like access to computer information between agencies or space to warehouse youth picked up during school hours, but the focus of the discussion would degenerate quickly when staff at the Juvenile Intervention Facility would bring up — again — how parents would often refuse to pick up a child at the end of the day. Once the youth were in custody, whose responsibility were they at 4:00 p.m.? And where were the parents anyway?

Soon, a dedicated few courageous souls began to meet separately to discuss "root cause" issues and create a root cause intake tool that would allow those working with youth to determine what was really going on in this kid's life that kept her or him out of school and moving toward an unhappy and possibly even dangerous future. Over the next few months, while still deeply involved in the weekly demands of the Task Force in general, on top of our own full-time professional commitments, our work group steadily uncovered many of the underlying factors at play for troubled youth.

We learned, for example, that a disproportionate number of truant youth were being badly abused or neglected either physically or emotionally at home or elsewhere. Some of them were struggling with the most basic needs of their lives going unmet. Some of them were going through crises, like the death of a parent, without any counseling or social support. Some of them lived in houses where drugs were more available than food, where no one had finished high school, where their comings and goings were not monitored, where they might be not only encouraged, but expected to participate in criminal activities.

We learned that children of mentally ill parents or guardians frequently are left to fend for themselves, sometimes even against the adults in their lives. We learned that children who exhibit psychological or emotional problems themselves quickly become frustrating or even overwhelming to parents or guardians who may have their own problems. We learned that children of addicts or alcoholics are four times more likely to become addicts, too. And that DJJ workers, who were often lacking in skills and education and paid as little as possible, sometimes perpetuate the youths' problems or even take them to a whole new level. The part-time school social workers available could not begin to address the sheer numbers involved, let alone the long-standing and far-reaching nature of the youths' physical, educational, psychological, and emotional difficulties.

In the face of all this, a couple of us were adamant about adding to the list an attempt to examine the effects of racial oppression on children of color and their families in school settings and in the greater society, as well. In the process of trying to draft the root cause intake tool, we haggled back and forth, hour after hour, making steady headway in every area except racism.

"You don't want to ask questions that start these kids looking for racism," one social worker on the committee studying root causes declared during one discussion. "That can create further tension where there might not really have been a problem."

"Would you avoid asking about things that might be going on at home because you might put something in a child's head?" I would counter. "You sound as if you don't believe that racism is present in Broward County or that it affects Black children in ways that keep them away from school."

I wanted desperately to say, "Don't you hear yourself? You're a perfect example of the problem. You're a White social service professional with decades of experience who genuinely wants to help kids, but you're still sweeping the issue of racism against Black children and Black families under the rug." Sometimes I just wanted to walk away from the table, but what kept me from doing so was the knowledge that there were particular days and particular meetings where those children had no other voice but mine. If it hadn't been for the selfless work of a highly intelligent and incredibly hard-working young, African-American school social worker, I might have buckled under the pressure. But I couldn't abandon her or the children and she wouldn't quit, so I couldn't either.

Ultimately, the root cause intake tool was drafted, including four questions calculated to identify any problems youth might be experiencing related to their race or any effects that had developed for them in that area. At various points in the questionnaire, the youth was asked to answer true or false:

"Kids at my school are friendly toward kids of my racial/ethnic/cultural group."

"The adults in my school show respect for people of my racial/ethnic/cultural group."

"People of my racial/ethnic/cultural group are usually successful."

"I am proud to be a member of my racial/ethnic/cultural group."

But when the questionnaire was printed and released for testing throughout the school system, it appeared without those four questions, even though no one had the right to make those changes without the agreement of the other committee members. I was livid and dismayed. The African-American social worker must have felt as if she'd been slapped in the face. She made the original version of the questionnaire available on request, but we both knew that the "official" version would receive the attention and that its testing would serve to give it social scientific and social service legitimacy that the version with "our" four questions would not enjoy.

Ultimately, all of our struggle in this direction only appeared publicly for posterity on page 13 of the Truancy Task Force Report, which was published in October of 1998. Tempers were running short with exhaustion. We were all tired of the verbal altercations that seemed to accompany every discussion. But I was still doggedly committed to seeing this process produce a deadly honest, reality-based product in the best interests of the children, our community, and the greater society, leaving out nothing. My opportunity to make good on my commitment came abruptly when the other members of the committee to write the report left a meeting table one afternoon with the announcement that I could just write it alone, which I proceeded to do. The Truancy Task Force and the Juvenile Justice Board of Broward County, Florida, eventually passed as item (a) under Recommendation Two of the Report:

> *"Cultural competence (the body of knowledge and skills necessary to interact with the members of any and all cultural groups as whole human beings worthy of respect) is an imperative expectation in any community that desires to establish safety and well-being for its residents. Broward County service providers must be committed to the process of becoming culturally competent."*

After months of deliberation and many hours of hard fought discussion, that was it. And I dropped out of the Task Force shortly after the Report's publication, trying to take solace in the fact that this simple statement would appear before all subsequent readers, including those in Tallahassee and Washington, D.C., though it wasn't nearly enough.

About this time, I was approached privately by Randi, during a break at one of the many, many meetings we were attending at this time. She sat down next to me on a stone bench outside the building in which we were located that day and leaned toward me as if to confide something she didn't want anyone else to hear. Her voice was hushed, but dramatic and somewhat contemptuous.

"I just came down in the elevator with some of the other social service professionals and you should hear how they talk about you," she began. "We're getting *really* tired of the way you're always pushing race, race, race like it's the only thing that matters. It's going to affect your career if you're not careful, you know..." And with that, she looked into my eyes meaningfully, stood up, and walked away.

1998

Randi was correct when she suggested to me that my stance was about to affect my career as a professional. It was only a matter of weeks before I received a call from Willie Myles, the founder and President of the largest Black social service agency in Broward County. An out-spoken member of the Juvenile Justice Board, Myles was unapologetically straight-forward when the need arose, as it often did, and even if he did not attend some committee meeting or other, he was always represented by knowledgeable African-American members of his staff.

He had named his agency Friends of Children, Youth, and Families, Inc., when he founded it seven years before, using a few thousand dollars from his personal savings account. His core staff, which had been with him from the beginning, when he couldn't even afford to pay them, was fiendishly loyal, markedly intelligent, and largely just as unapologetic as he was.

"Are you happy where you are?" he began with the classic recruitment question.

I changed phones to increase my privacy and asked him what he meant.

"Well," he continued. "We've been watching you for some time and listening to what you say. We're very impressed with your consistency. You always say the same things no matter what setting you're in. We think there might be a place for you at Friends of Children."

My brain was rushing hard. It's always an ego-boost to have someone you respect approach you like this, but there were elements of this opportunity that were so exciting to me and such a tremendous honor under the circumstances of my Whiteness, that I was stunned.

I knew what he meant by "consistency." Most White people talk quite differently depending on the racial make-up of whatever group they are in at the time, whether or not they intend to. Not only do they often speak one way to African-Americans and a different way to other White folks, but even those who sound very liberal or even radical when involved in private conversations with Black people will typically speak differently when one or more other Whites are present. While Willie Myles and his staff could not be sure of what I said behind closed doors (where everyone was White), they knew that I pushed a hard-core anti-racist agenda around them, even when Whites were present.

It was a very smart move on his part to recruit me. Friends of Children had at least fifteen programs at that point, both residential and non-residential, with close to one hundred workers and a multi-million dollar budget provided both contractually and by grant funding. Not only had I been baptized by fire working directly with troubled youth myself in Miami, but I already knew the whole Florida DJJ training curriculum, I was familiar with the grant funding process from the inside, and I had connections throughout the system state-wide. It was a no-brainer.

On the other hand, from my perspective, here was an opportunity for me as an anti-racist White person to join a truly remarkable group of Afri-centric men and women of color to write grant proposals, rather than just evaluate, review, and monitor them, and to help design programs intended to undermine institutionalized oppression against Black children. Shoot! I would have taken a cut in pay to make the shift! So, when Myles asked me what I was making and offered me a substantial raise in salary, I accepted his offer instantly, thinking I had surely died and gone to activist Heaven.

As it turned out, I stayed with Friends of Children for two years and it most assuredly was *not* Heaven. For starters, three days after I joined the staff, the edict went out that the agency would be going to uniforms: executive level women would be wearing black suits and teal shells with the option of wearing pants or skirts. I was speechless. When I first heard it, I said to Myles' sister, Mary, who was to become a bosom friend and ally during my years with the agency, "You can't be serious."

Myles came to my office within the hour.

"Tell me the truth," he said. "Would you have come with us if you'd known three days ago that we were going to make this change?"

"I'd wear a chicken suit, if you wanted me to," I responded without hesitation. "But you must make sure that men and women are treated the same on this thing or you're going to get the wrong kind of attention for it."

Soon, workers throughout the agency were in teal and black everywhere. Polo shirts with logos for the direct service staff. Suits further up the line. And black shoes on everyone. We looked like an army. And I had to smile. I remembered IBM when it first moved to Boca Raton in the 1960s. They hired a man I knew and it was the first time I had ever heard of a company requiring particular dress on its office staff. As a junior executive, my friend had to wear a dress shirt and tie everyday with either a sport coat or a cardigan sweater, which could only be blue or grey. We thought it was fixated. But at Friends of Children, it was genius.

At the first Florida Department of Juvenile Justice state conference we went to in our "colors," we came down the halls of the hotel like a cadre of gangbusters. I had rarely been prouder at any time in my life and I had never felt more a part of an important effort than I did striding into a meeting room with four or five African-American co-workers, all of us in black, taking care of business, taking care of children, representing Myles. I can't see the movie "Men in Black" to this day without thinking of Friends of Children. I wore a black suit and teal shell every workday for two years and never regretted a moment of it.

The plan initially was for me to report to the Vice President, a man who had been hired to take some of the horrendous day-to-day pressure off of Willie Myles. I don't know whether or not Myles, who had great confidence in me and ruled his agency with an iron hand, ever considered the possibility that his staff would be less pleased with his acquisition than he was. In actuality, I was never totally accepted at Friends of Children. There were always pockets of resistance which might crop up when I least expected it and often looked like it was something other than personal, but I always knew.

The first series of dramas involved the Vice President, who may have felt threatened by my presence, though I had no designs on his job. I didn't need to. I didn't want to be an administrator. I wanted to design programs and get them funded, set them up and move on to the next proposal. I wanted to train people how to save kids. I wanted to stay on top of all the late-breaking research on troubled children.

And I wanted to provide Willie Myles with the inside scoop on whatever information I might become privy to as I went around the county. I wanted, in short, to do exactly what I have been hired to do.

But, from day one, the VP made my life miserable. He was rude, he was aggressive, he was sneaky, and he was insulting. He would make massive and picayune demands on my time and energy. He would try to trip me up into embarrassing myself. And he would do all this while gliding up and down the halls as if on wheels, his oily smile striking chills into my heart.

I was only supervising one man at this time, a man that was hired to fill a program slot I had developed and gotten funded for Myles even before I was actually on board at the agency. The worker was in the field most of the time as a case manager for youth with addiction problems, so I didn't see him a great deal, but as best I could tell, he wasn't doing what he was being paid to do. He started late, he wasn't keeping paperwork to establish his accountability, and he talked to me as if he owed me no explanation and no respect. I tried to suggest to Myles that I thought the man was lying about his work, but Myles, not understanding what was going on, referred me to my supervisor.

Between the VP and the man under me, I was soon feeling a debilitating level of stress most of the time I was at work. When the VP finally realized what an opportunity he had in my underling to squeeze me even more, he called a meeting for the three of us where he allowed the worker to castigate me mercilessly while the VP refused to let me answer him at all. By the time he finished with me, I was in tears and raging, but when I told Mary what had happened and that I was on the verge of leaving my position, she advised me to lay low.

A few minutes later, Willie Myles himself entered my office and told me simply that I would now be reporting directly to him. Apparently, he had overheard the interchange during the meeting that afternoon and he was acting to ensure that it would not occur again. Ultimately, the VP got caught in a string of lies and even stole several thousand dollars from Friends of Children in an attempt to set up his own agency. And my underling was found to be having an affair on company time with another agency employee, who was married to somebody else. So they were both fired. Nevertheless, from that first incident onward, I think Myles was forced to accept that the men and women of color who worked at his agency might kowtow to him as the force that he was — both personally and professionally — but they were not going to accept his choice of me in the way that he had hoped and maybe honestly believed that they would.

He was disappointed, I think, and it played out as disappointment in me. Mary suggested on more than one occasion that he had hoped to groom me for a position higher up in the organization, but that he was no longer sure I could handle it. In point of fact, he hired two more Vice Presidents while I was working for him — both Black, both flashy, both expensive, and both disastrous for Friends of Children. I could hardly have done worse. But many, probably most, of his employees never did get what in the world Myles was thinking when he put me in place in the agency at all. I was White, for God's sake, and when push came to shove, they didn't appreciate having me up in their space any more than people in the Black clubs in Tallahassee had. There were plenty of other agencies in Broward County where I could work. Why did I want to force my way into this one? And even if Willie Myles wanted me, they seemed to communicate as often as possible, why did I have to accept?

One of my co-workers explained early on that the tension was all about "entropy," the steady and inevitable deterioration of a society growing directly out of whatever dynamics were in play at its inception. In other words, that we were all — Black or White — just caught inescapably in the mesh of our shared history and that this would make it impossible for us to communicate adequately or live together comfortably. But we wound up exchanging books, he moved on eventually, and I clung to my beliefs — or at least my hopes — that I could, in fact, be useful, if not fit in.

Finally, at a meeting to plan a special all-day event of some kind, I came to realize in a much more practical way what my co-worker had meant. There were probably six or seven of us gathered around a conference table to come up with ideas and hash out details for the event. Everyone else at the table was Black, of course. I had been around for long enough, well over a year, at least, that I no longer thought much about it myself in spite of the reminders that would usually come in the form of someone expressing surprise that I knew who Shep and the Limelites were or had asked for a second helping of collard greens at an agency affair.

In any case, I sat at the table, listening to the rapid-fire discussion, the ideas bouncing back and forth like ping pong balls, but I couldn't get a word in edgewise to save my life. Brian would say something and Kwame might answer. Mary would chime in her two cents and the others would agree or disagree, make a suggestion or develop a thought, but it was as if I wasn't there. I not only couldn't get my ideas across, I couldn't even get the others' attention. I raised my hand. I cleared my throat. I tapped the table. I tried to boldly interrupt. Nothing worked. My frustration level became apoplectic. And all of a sudden, I got it. *This* is what African-Americans feel like all the time, I thought to myself, at tables where *they* are the only one representing *their* "race."

The realization hit me like a brick. It hit me so hard that I had to lay my forehead down on the table in front of me for a minute just to re-group. When I raised my head, I no longer tried to intervene until I was asked. And I was. I didn't feel as if they were trying to be rude. I didn't believe for a minute they were trying to ignore me. Years of Black people and White people sitting at different tables, having separate conversations, had created a scenario where we were simply in different worlds. Being at this table on this day with these particular people had reduced me to equality, that's all, had made me *unnecessary* to the conversation, had placed me in the precise position to which people of color are usually relegated when White folks are talking — on the outside of the circle.

It was similar to the time I spent with the Sudanese refugees in Toronto when I was not held to be more important than anyone else, when I was not granted due privilege or treated with deference, and when I responded ultimately by becoming *furious* at other people. But this time, again reduced to equality, I was choking, instead, on my own frustration and absolutely overwhelmed by my desire to be included, to be recognized, to be other than invisible. Within days, I knew that I would eventually write it all down as I have now done.

I earned my keep at Friends of Children, and I will always hope that the core team who has continued to remain there thinks of me with half of the fondness with which I think of them. But Willie Myles gave me far more than a salary and a place to make a difference. He gave me an opportunity to be re-educated, however slightly, to have at least a *little* of my Whiteness rubbed off, to make it possible for me to see a little more clearly what it is to be Black or White in the United States and what it feels like when Black people and White people make the honorable attempt to be allies.

While I was struggling through the realization of my own racial identity issues, Morgan was, too, I learned one afternoon without warning. She and I were sitting side by side on the couch in our living room in Ft. Lauderdale, having moved to a little Florida-style stucco house with a screened-in porch and white tile floors and ceiling fans. We loved it and it was in a neighborhood that she had very much lobbied to move into, near a school she had wanted to attend where most of her friends, it appeared to me, were White. I had long since gotten over trying to talk with her about race. So her comment caught me completely off-guard. She was in the middle of telling me some kind of story when she interrupted herself to describe the setting, "*You* know how a buncha White folks get when they're all together in a room and they get uptight..."

I was stunned. My head jerked to the right so I could look at her face. She was still deep into her story and wasn't even looking at me. If she had made the statement for effect, I couldn't tell it. But the grin on my face eventually got her attention. Given her unwillingness to talk seriously about race and my own excitement at her crack about "White folks" as an indicator that she had, indeed, found a space for herself as a young bi-racial woman, I didn't want to spoil the moment by saying anything. Still, I couldn't help the grin.

When she finally acknowledged my facial expression, I looked at her as if to say, "White folks, huh?" And she laughed a laugh I had been waiting for all of her life.

"Well, you *do* know..." she said. And I did.

PART SIX

2001

I left Friends of Children the summer following my son, Eli's, death from a hot shot of heroin a rival gangbanger had slipped him in February of 2000. His long-term addiction had finally succeeded in killing him early one Friday morning while his friends tried desperately and unsuccessfully to save his life until the ambulance could arrive. The telephone call from the police had sent me to the floor like a falling tree, only faster. I spent most of the call lying on my side, lifting my head off the floor, berating the officer indignantly.

"Is this the *only* way you could think of to tell me that my *son* is dead — over the **telephone**?!" I squawked.

The officer apologized, explaining that they hadn't been sure I was the one they should notify. Because Eli had already been identified by his friends, the morgue wouldn't even allow me to see his body, though they did show me a photograph. And so my precious first-born child left the earth unexpectedly one day two weeks before his twenty-third birthday, leaving Morgan and me behind. It was the beginning of a year of losses for me.

In July, I left Friends of Children to strike out on my own. I had a couple of contracts to start out with and was newly married, so I figured that it would be okay if things got off to a slow start. Then my husband and I bought a house in Sunrise, so I left the home that Morgan and I had shared for five years, a home where I had been, by and large, fairly happy most of the time. In August, while I was taking our furniture from one house to the other, Morgan moved to Tampa to work on a Bachelor's Degree at the University of South Florida. Even my car died that year and had to be replaced by one I liked infinitely less, though it was a better car.

By New Year's Day, 2001, I was in a different house, a different car, a different job, and without either my son or my daughter. When my husband admitted to me that he had not only been unfaithful, but had been intentionally cruel to me ever since in hopes that I would leave him, I gave up and walked away. As soon as the summer semester closed and the courses I was teaching ended, I gathered up what little I had accumulated over the years and got the heck out of Dodge, following Morgan to Tampa by default.

I had just used a credit card to pay her August rent. So, I reasoned that I had a right to live with her for the remainder of that month in any case. Besides, rent was cheaper in Tampa, and though Morgan had been talking about moving into student housing, I knew that, on my own, I would not be able to assist her financially other than to offer her a radically cheap rent arrangement. She reluctantly agreed and we took a two-bedroom apartment, which tossed us back into each other's lives in a way neither of us had bargained for and neither of us welcomed.

Nevertheless, I was almost immediately hired for a position as a social service administrator and began teaching at USF, as well. By down-sizing my life and my car and carefully budgeting my money over the next few years, I was able to make a dent in the financial disaster that leaving my marriage had produced for me. And, as it turned out, Morgan and I — stuck with each other and with only each other for much of the time — managed eventually to work through much of our mother/daughter angst by the time she graduated and moved away from me once more.

When the Sociology Department chair at USF asked me if I would be willing to teach "Racial and Ethnic Relations" in the spring of 2003, I was excited at the prospect. I had taught the course once before at Florida Atlantic University, but it had been at least several years earlier and I wondered what my years of experience at Friends of Children might have added to my presentation of the subject. Part of the process of working for Willie Myles had involved participating in an on-going series of rigorous trainings on Afri-centricity, being exposed to a continual focus on Afri-centric rather than Euro-centric perspectives, and, for that matter, being inundated by Blackness itself on a daily basis, none of which were targeted particularly at me, but all of which took me on pretty much the ride of a middle class White woman's life. I had relished it all — every moment, every conversation, every recommended book, every correction of a misunderstood idea. If they were willing to teach me, I was willing to learn.

So, I knew that the course was very likely to be electric. I had plenty to say and knew I was willing to say it, even if it made students crazy. I might not get the opportunity again and I was going to do my teachers proud.

When another professor suggested that I could use Joe R. Feagin's <u>Racist America</u> as my principle text book for the course, I looked it over and chose it immediately. I had met Joe a decade before when I invited him to come to Florida State to talk about the book he had most recently published at that time. I found him to be erudite and certainly anti-racist, but very down-to-earth, as well, and I was glad to be able to support his newest book. Then I added two other books and a whole series of intensely provocative videos to the line-up.

Each class period, I had my students view a carefully selected film calculated to get them all worked up right before class ended and I sent them home to write a reflection on what they had learned from it. Then, in following weeks, I would read some of the most challenging and thought-provoking reflections to the class without identifying the student writers. This made it possible to give them a voice without watching our very limited class hours be eaten up with argumentative protests based primarily on racist perceptions. It also allowed them to say what was really on their minds without having to worry about how other students might receive their thoughts.

I like interspersing dramatic works and poems here and there during my lectures and unabashedly tweak my students' feelings in a variety of ways that help them break through to a deeper understanding of social realities they may not otherwise be able to imagine.

"Whenever I see a fifty-year-old Black man on a bicycle ridin' down the edge of the street on a hot day goin' in the opposite direction while I'm in my car with the A/C pumpin' and the sound system rockin' out," I might say forcefully and with emotion, "when his eyes meet mine, I can't help but think that he didn't pick up that bike to get a little *exercise. He'd* like to have a car, *too,* but African-American men are four times more likely to be unemployed than White American men at *every educational level.* And even the ones who are allowed to *get* a job make roughly three-fourths of what a White man would get to do the same job. How do you suppose he *feels* about having to ride a *bicycle* at the age of fifty while *I'm* in my little red *car*? And how do you suppose he *feels* about *me*?"

Even the students of color get in touch with things they might otherwise have long since started trying to avoid thinking about.

"In all oppressive situations," wrote Calvin Hernton in The Sexual Mountain and Black Women Writers,[i] "it is deemed a virtue for the oppressed to identify with the world-view of the oppressors. The oppressed are 'praised' and 'rewarded' for loathing themselves and for admiring their oppressors; they are derided, made to feel ashamed, and are punished for embracing any ways they themselves might develop, and are *instructed* and *forced* to manifest allegiance to the ways of those who oppress them." But not in *my* class. I look to set people free...even myself.

As a matter of fact, I agree with Paulo Friere in The Pedagogy of the Oppressed: "There is no such thing as a neutral educational process. Education either functions as an instrument which is used to facilitate the integration of the younger generation into the logic of the present system and bring about conformity to it, or it becomes the practice of freedom, the means by which men and women deal critically and creatively with reality and discover how to participate in the transformation of their world."[ii]

I believe that education is an inter-relational experience during which the conscious presence of both the teacher and the student is required. Even when I'm standing in front of the class talking, the students in front of me determine the course of my delivery process. A question, a curious eye, a sorrowful gaze, a skeptical frown, a quixotic smile, an angry demeanor, can all change my direction at a moment's notice without the student even knowing it. I want my practice of education to be a practice of freedom. I want my students to discover how to participate in the transformation of our world. Because otherwise, as the late Jamaican reggae artist, Bob Marley, sang, "Until the philosophy which holds one race superior and another inferior is finally and permanently discredited and abandoned, everywhere is war...Until there no longer are first class and second class citizens of any nation, until the color of a man's skin is of no more significance than the color of his eyes, there is war."

Hernton, Friere, and Marley all sound so in agreement because there was slavery in the so-called "New World" for far longer than we have been without it (slavery was made illegal only 160 years ago, while the former period lasted for over 250 years). But it is also true that the on-going impact of institutionalized oppression in the form of racism has continued through the handing down of cultural norms and perceptions throughout U.S. society to the present. When I ask my students to write down what they learned — one way or the other — about other ethnic and racial groups when they were growing up (in the 1990s), they invariably list the same kinds of stereotypes, semester after semester, that would have appeared on a similarly requested list in the 1950s or before.

One class's compiled list had them admitting that, when they were children, they learned that African-Americans are "poor, lazy, loud, stupid, irresponsible and violent, weed-smoking liars, thieves and gang-members, who are more likely to be on welfare, love to eat fried chicken, and are troublemakers from the ghetto who are always late, beg for stuff, have no sense of self, and are drug-addicted criminal trash who live a hard life because they choose to...!" Even if someone wanted to argue that these students all learned when they grew up that these stereotypes were not true, we would still have to remember that those who taught them all this were themselves taught the same things and then grew up, many of them, to see, work with, know, and even love people of color who are nothing at all like any of those stereotypes. So if growing up and learning differently makes the stereotypes go away, then why were they still around for these kids to learn?

When I further encourage my students to carry an index card around for a week, making a slash mark every time they hear, see, or think a reference to race or ethnicity, they are startled to find that we think about racial and ethnic issues all day long — a conservative estimated average of at least 45,000 times in their first twenty years! Considering the pejorative nature of the above list and imagining those kinds of stereotypes lathered that many times over one person's brain, it's no wonder we're all so hyper-racialized. And as Jane Elliott, whose consciousness-raising experiments using eye color to demonstrate the effects of racial discrimination, often says, "It's not the intent; it's the *impact*." The fact that we are basically good people who mean well means diddley-squat (as my mother used to say), if the damage done is brutal, insistent, and on-going.

As I prepared for the first day of class that semester, though, I wanted to do something really special in the classroom, something that would immediately excite the students to the level of what they might learn in the course, if they liked it, and make them want to drop the course, if they were not ready for it. I didn't see much point in watching some White youth slouched in the back of the classroom for the duration, giving me the evil eye while grinding his or her teeth week after week to the point of ulcers. And I wanted very badly to start out with a strong statement, to communicate that we were going to boldly examine racial and ethnic relations; White privilege, in general; and

Black/White relations, in particular, as if our lives and futures depended on it.

Then it occurred to me. I would have the class put themselves into a giant circle in skin-tone order. I told Morgan what I was going to do and she immediately committed herself to be there, which was very uncharacteristic of her. She had seen me "perform" in the classroom for years and she had her own busy schedule, as well, but this, she said, was something she wanted to see, as long as the others would not be told that she was my daughter.

When I walked into the room for the class, I was somewhat unsettled because there were about sixty students and the room looked to be disproportionately filled with people of color. I didn't know how this was going to affect the exercise and I was more concerned that a person of color might be offended by the exercise than a White person, who would probably be too embarrassed to admit their discomfort, in any case. I was keenly aware that the perception of an offense of that nature could cost me the opportunity to teach. Consequently, I was seriously nervous. In fact, Morgan told me later that, at first, I was *so* nervous, I was talking with some kind of accent!

Anyway, I was committed. We had gotten through the first half of the class, took a break, and, for good or ill, I was ready to proceed. From the moment I began the exercise, I kept up a constant banter. I believed — rightly or wrongly — that this first time through, at least, if I didn't maintain control of the group, things might quickly degenerate in ways I could not repair.

First, I talked about how the socially-constructed political notion of "race" is not biological. In the late 1940s and early 1950s, in fact, the United Nations Educational, Scientific, and Cultural Organization (UNESCO) brought together eminent scientific minds from all over the world to study the concept of race. After several years of rigorous analysis, they determined that "'race' is not so much a biological phenomenon, as a social myth," and that, if there had ever been separate and distinct races before, they certainly had not persisted into the mid-1900s. Apparently, I went on, there is no way to identify a drop of blood as being from a "Black" person or a "White" person under normal circumstances.

Then I pointed out that we have no idea, when looking at a person, whether or not they have African-American ancestry. White people want to think we can tell, but we can't, especially not after a couple of generations and particularly not if the blood-line has been crossed with that of one or more alternative ethnicities. "Tiger" Woods, for example, is only one-quarter African-American and Colin Powell's background through his Jamaican immigrant parents has strong European, Jewish, and Indian strains. Their descendants may sooner than later look very little different from typical "White" people, regardless of their heritage as people of color, but our current social norms would still categorize them as "Black," even if that occurred.

An additional and even more dramatic example is Gregory Howard Williams, whose book <u>Life on the Color Line: The True Story of a White Boy Who Discovered He Was Black</u>,[iii] describes how he suddenly lost all the privileges of his Whiteness at ten-years-old even though he looks as White as any White man I've ever seen.

"Who wants to guess what *my* racial category is?" I asked the group boldly, looking from face to face, challenging them to take a risk.

"*No* one?" I pushed. "Why not? I have very light skin and straight hair...but you're not *absolutely* sure I'm 'White,' are you? As a matter of fact, how can *I* be sure beyond a shadow of a doubt what I am?"

And turning to the White students, I added, "Or *you*, for that matter?"

Nevertheless, I continued, the socially-constructed political notion of race is the principle social identifier in the United States and we make our judgments based on a perception that we can always biologically ascertain racial identity. I reminded them that, in spite of the conclusions of the UNESCO scientists to the contrary more than sixty years ago, we have well-established scholars who *still* maintain that race is biological, and that even some sociology texts define race as a category indicated by skin tone and hair texture, ignoring the fact that Gregory Williams' experience would prove otherwise. Periodically, I went on, we even have some so-called "scientist" pop up and declare that their "research" proves that people of color are biologically inferior in one way or another to Whites. And though their "findings" are invariably eventually debunked, their publications remain on library shelves without disclaimer. Then I told them that I wanted them to put themselves in skin tone order.

The eyebrows went up and the students started milling around, making soft noises and appearing visibly uncomfortable. I used myself as an example, comparing arms with some of the students to find my "position." I told them to form a large circle and find their place in it. I enlisted the other students' aid in assisting a blind student (a light-skinned Black man) to find where he "belonged" and insisted that the African-American students (who were clumped up at the "dark end" of the circle, resisting the declaration of a specific position) thin their line to one-person deep.

I encouraged the group by telling them that there were going to be dollars handed out shortly and that they must be one-person deep in order to determine who would get the cash. That seemed to help. We even had to deal with the presence of a White student in a wheel chair who could not get easily through the maze of desks. We estimated where he would fit and then had students go over to him and compare arms until we found his "slot." By now, they had made peace with the process and exhaled somewhat, though most of the White students looked a little flat-faced (with small, pasty-looking smiles and nervous eyes) while the Black students were clearly reserving judgment and maybe waiting for the other shoe to fall, presented with what they might have seen at that point as one crazy White woman who was obviously liable to do anything.

Moving around the inside of the circle to a White student who was about three people away from where "color" started to appear, I asked her, "When you have to check a box on a form, what do you check to indicate which group you identify yourself with?"

"White," she replied matter-of-factly.

"And you?" I asked the woman next to her.

"White," she also replied.

"And how about you?" I asked the next woman, who didn't look radically different from the other two, but looked as if she might be from another country.

"Where I come from," she fired back strongly, "we don't think that's anybody else's business! I don't check a box at *all*!"

The African-American students looked startled and somewhat pleased, like they were impressed with her answer and liked such a thought. I jumped on it quickly.

"You see?" I queried. "Some cultures don't force individuals to constantly racialize themselves. Why does ours?"

I proceeded on around the circle, pointing out that we were listing in order: White, White, no answer, Black, White, Latino, Latino, Black, Latino, Asian...

"How can race be biological," I asked the group, "if we can't draw clear lines of demarcation? Shouldn't all the Blacks be in one section of the circle and all the Whites in another? Shouldn't everybody in a category look alike?"

Then I took a deep breath, looked around the room, and said, "Okay...now we're going to add 'hair texture' as a secondary identifier."

You could see the African-American students' eyes go to half-mast.

"Just bear with me," I said seriously, looking straight at them. "We're learning something here..."

The White students remained pleasant, if somewhat numb-looking. Nobody moved. I never hesitated, walking over to a Latino man with wavy hair who looked at me as if he wished he could disappear.

"Now," I continued brightly, indicating various students as I went along, "how can we clearly define ourselves or each other when we've got this man who calls himself a 'Latino' standing next to a woman that identifies herself as 'Asian?' His hair is wavy and hers is straight, but her skin is darker than his. Which one should come first: lighter skin with wavy hair or darker skin with smoother hair? And what are we going to do with a woman who comes *before* him in the skin tone continuum, but identifies herself as 'Black' and has *some* curl in her hair, but who comes *after* a Latino woman whose skin is even lighter, but whose hair is *very* curly?"

By this time, they were right with me and I was moving at a good speed. Whipping six one-dollar bills out of my brief case, I handed one bill to each of the six students with the darkest skin and then looked around the circle without comment. The other students looked crest-fallen.

"*Oh*," I said. "You're disappointed you didn't get dollars, too? How does that feel — *not* getting a dollar, when *they* got a dollar?"

"I feel like I'm in the wrong place," responded one light-skinned Latino woman immediately. I repeated her words back to the group and added, "So, we don't like it when other people get rewarded for being in a quasi-biological category that we're not a part of, huh?"

I repeated my original question again, slowly and clearly: "How do we *feel* when someone else gets a dollar and we don't when the decision made is based on something neither they nor we have any control over?"

The student with the darkest skin in the room chortled, "I don't know!" and everybody laughed. But I was able to add just before releasing them for the day, "In our society, White people have come to expect — and do not even know they are getting — special privileges and rewards all their lives just because their skin tone categorizes and identifies them as 'White.' People of color know it and are hurt by it, but do not have the power to change it. This semester, should you decide to return, we will consider what this does to us, to our society, and to our futures. See you next week!"

And I did — almost every one of them.

---

[i] The Sexual Mountain and Black Women Writers by Calvin C. Hernton (NY: Anchor Press/Doubleday, 1987, p. 83)

[ii] Gramschi, Freire, and Adult Education: Possibilities for Transformative Action by Peter Mayo (Macmillan, 1999, p. 5)

[iii] Life on the Color Line: The True Story of a White Boy Who Discovered He Was Black by Gregory Howard Williams (Plume, 1996)

2004

After several semesters teaching the course, challenging my students to declare the racial category into which they would place me, I began to consider the possibility that I might, in fact, have African-American roots somewhere back in my family heritage. When my daughter was young, she had once assured me that I wasn't "White," anyway — I was "peach-colored." It was some years later before I realized that referring to skin-tone in various food-related colors is common in the African-American community. Cinnamon, chocolate, lemon-colored, brown sugar, honey pecan — the list is as long as the imagination. I had been introduced more than once by a Black acquaintance to another African-American person as "not *really* White." And had been taunted by some for my full lower lip, my prominent backside, and a dark spot on my leg that was about the size of a dime.

But none of that indicated any real likelihood as to what my racial background might actually be. I was intrigued by the idea. I thought it would make a powerful moment in my class, if I could announce to my students' consternation that their White-looking professor was "Black." I became almost fixated, poring over the internet genealogy websites for hours on end. Besides, I had been thinking about writing a book on race ever since working for Friends of Children. What a great addition to the book it would be, I thought, to describe how I had discovered the one drop of Black blood that makes me Black!

I had never been able to intellectually understand my fascination with race. It made no sense, really. My parents were neither dyed-in-the-wool liberals nor openly rabid racists. My experiences as a child were relatively middle of the road for a young girl raised in northern Illinois. I hadn't gone out of my way to avoid being a part of the White community. And I hadn't immersed myself utterly in Black America. "Why do I hope I'm Black?" I asked myself.

I tried putting intellectual parameters on the feeling. Maybe I was so aggressively anti-racist, I reasoned, that I wanted to shed my "Whiteness," and identify myself physically with the oppressed group, once and for all. Maybe I was being driven by some undeniable spiritual compunction to uncover a deep-seated truth about my self or my family. Or maybe I was just a drama-queen, I thought, never satisfied until I can trump my last "act." But it hardly mattered, I ultimately admitted to myself. I couldn't stop the process. I lived on the internet week-end after week-end, chasing the one Black drop.

My daughter was less than supportive.

"*Mom*," she declared with more than a hint of disdain in her voice, "finding an African-American ancestor in your family won't make you *Black*! If you've never been followed around in a store while you're trying to shop, you're not *Black*, no matter what your bloodline says!"

I knew from listening to my students and other African-American people over the years that this would be an attitude held by many people of color. Nevertheless, I had seen enough very, very light-skinned "Blacks" to know that, if I declared myself "Black" and stuck by it and could document that I was directly descended from a person of color, I could create one hell of a discussion on "race." And it was a discussion I wanted to create. I wanted other "White" people to look at me and have to imagine that they, too, might have a "drop" of African blood. I knew that such a demonstration would work to undermine the White rationale for mandated privilege. How could we rightly claim the benefits of our "superiority" if we didn't even know which of us "deserve" it and which do not?

I searched and I searched. I followed endless threads of historical accounts, started haunting genealogical message boards, and pored over the U.S. census records till my eyes blurred, burned, and watered. And still no direct connection. I did find a number of "Black," "colored," and "mulatto" people named "White" (my mother's maiden name) listed in the 1870 and 1880 census results for Clay County, Kentucky, where I was born, but there appeared to be no way for me to ascertain whether or not I was related to any of them.

Then, chasing down yet another historical lead on the internet, I found a 1995 article by Dwight Billings and Kathleen Blee (sociologists themselves), entitled "Agriculture and Poverty in the Kentucky Mountains: Beech Creek and Clay County, 1850-1910."[i] And on page six, I found the following:

> *"James White, a Virginian whose estate was valued at $2 million when he died in 1838, began to purchase land and manufacture salt in Clay County in*

cooperation with his brother Hugh White (and Hugh's sons), who moved to Clay County during the first decade of the nineteenth century. By 1860, the White family controlled approximately 20,000 acres of land in Clay and other mountain counties. James Garrard, the second governor of Kentucky, patented more than 45,000 acres of land in Kentucky before and after Kentucky became a state. Although most of his lands were in the Blue Grass region, Garrard also bought thousands of acres in southeastern Kentucky and sent his son Daniel to Clay County to establish salt wells and furnaces there early in the century. The Whites and the Garrards, along with a few other families, thus established economic and political dynasties in Clay County based on slave labor, salt manufacturing, commerce, and large-scale farming that persisted throughout the antebellum and early postbellum periods...The county's fifty-eight slaveowners, representing only 7 percent of household heads, owned 10 percent of the population (515 slaves) ...The ten wealthiest individuals in Clay County in 1860 — all of them slaveowners — averaged personal estates worth $45,890 in a county where the mean estate was worth only $859, or fifty-three times less."

Later in the article, it got even more specific, describing how "salt manufacturers Daugherty White, Alexander White, and James White, Sr....[held a] combined 80 slaves and Daniel and Theophilis Garrard [held]...21 slaves." The words felt like a flat wooden board smashing into my astonished face. I reeled under the weight of the knowledge. It took little exploration to verify that I was indeed related to all of the men the sociologists named, that Hugh Lowry White and Daniel Garrard were my great-great-great-great-grandfathers on my mother's side, and that I was descended from slaveholders.

It was unimaginable to me. I retreated into a shell of disbelief. My ears rang with silence like the horrible hush after an automatic weapon is shot. My body rejected food. I was incredulous.

"Well, what did you *expect*?" asserted Morgan ruthlessly. "You were *born* in Kentucky, for God's sake."

"I'm from the *mountains*," I countered dejectedly. "I vaguely knew there was money back there somewhere, but *slaveholding*...I mean, it's not like they had plantations in Clay County..."

"Whatever!" she tossed back at me, leaving me to my misery.

And I *was* miserable. For several weeks, I continued my searches for more information, now horrified in advance at what I might find, but incapable of stopping my forages for the truth. I could hardly face my African-American friends, students, and clients at work. I was convinced that they would retreat from me if they knew, backing silently away as one might from someone with a debilitating and contagious disease. I wasn't sure they wouldn't rail at me with angry words. I feared they might even punch me in the face, a reaction I would almost have welcomed under the circumstances of my own inability to come to grips with my new knowledge. Whenever I wasn't consciously caught up in the needs of the moment at work or at home, I mulled over the facts of my heritage. When I would least expect it, the refrain would waft into my head like an old spiritual song gone awry, "Slaves aaa-nd slaveholders...comin' for to carry me home...."

I finally took the plunge one afternoon with one of my clients — an elderly African-American woman. I started by telling her about the book I wanted to write and then described what I had discovered. I think, in retrospect, I was asking her for absolution. And I feel quite sure that she knew it. She was old and she was Black and Black people have been saving White people from their nightmares since the earliest days of slavery. My anguish notwithstanding, I had no right to present the matter to her and make her responsible for accepting it with grace. African-Americans have been forced for the past five hundred years to take up Whitey's slack, to respond with dignity however painful it is, to "understand" the unacceptable, to forgive the unforgivable, in the interest of being free from their own dark past. Still, I was helpless in the face of my dilemma. I could not easily go forward with my life, continuing to do my work, dragging this secret along behind me like so many bodies wrapped in chains and attached — now — permanently to my psyche.

She received my confession with the countenance of the priest I was begging her to be, nodding gently as the words proceeded with great hesitation from my quivering lips.

"You write your book," she finally pronounced by way of benediction. "You write your book and you tell your story and you do whatever it is God has for you to do."

And then she hugged me before she left, but not without a certain holding back. Or maybe that was just me, still feeling that no one from my family would ever deserve a hug from anyone again.

* * *

Over the next year, I followed my intellectual curiosity from point to point as if I was rigorously and dispassionately researching some topic for a scholarly paper. But in truth, my burning desire to look at the reality of it all held me in its thrall, rather like being unable not to gawk at the scene of a bloody accident as you pass it on a highway. I started by learning about Kentucky.

I had known for decades that Kentucky was a slave state; that, in fact, it had expressly bred slaves like a product, but now I took a closer look at the mindset that would be required to do such a thing. The historical record was graphic and predictable. Even before Kentucky became a state in 1792, declaring that slavery would be legal there, more than sixteen percent of its population was already made up of enslaved Africans and their descendants. By 1800, the Kentucky General Assembly had codified the institutionalized oppression by passing a whole string of laws calculated to make sure that even *free* Blacks would know that in Kentucky they were considered "inferior" and would not, for example, be allowed to vote. To underscore the generalized concern about free Blacks, then, in 1818, they were barred from moving into the state at all, and in 1851, those who had been born free in the state or freed while living there were unapologetically ordered to leave.

By 1850, Georgia, Virginia, and Kentucky shared the dubious distinction of having the most slaveholders in the nation, with twenty-five percent of Kentucky's population being slaves, and with 2,500 to 4,000 slaves being exported south every year as a three million dollar boost to the state's annual economy. Moreover, when the Emancipation Proclamation freed the slaves in the states that had seceded from the Union, it didn't affect Kentucky because she hadn't joined the Confederacy, so Kentucky's slaves remained in bondage until the end of the War more than two years later. Consistent with this unwillingness to follow others' leads, Kentucky's General Assembly maintained an unblemished record of rejecting the earliest attempts to recognize the rights of African-Americans, even after the War was over and even though Kentucky had not seceded.

In the five years immediately following the end of the Civil War, for instance, while most of the rest of the nation ratified the 13th, 14th, and 15th Amendments to the U.S. Constitution, freeing African-Americans from slavery and giving them full rights as citizens, including the right to vote, Kentucky successively rejected ratification of all three until March 18, 1976. And as if to emphasize her intentions during those earliest days after the War, Kentucky had lynchings occurring on the average of one per month between 1865 and 1875. It's no wonder that, by 1920, African-Americans made up less than 10% of Kentucky's overall population. Freed, they had moved out in droves, sometimes selling what little they had, including hard-bought family plots of land, to do so.

Interestingly enough, on the other hand, Kentucky somehow produced a few remarkable individuals who did not demonstrate the same ways of thinking. One of these was the Rev. John Fee, who founded the now-famous Berea College in 1855 in the mountains near where I was born. A well-known abolitionist, Fee established the institution on the premise that, despite the policies and practices of Kentucky and the rest of the nation, "God has made of one blood all the peoples of the earth." Local racists literally ran Fee out of the mountains, but after the War, he returned, recalcitrant, and soon, students such as Carter G. Woodson (the scholar who eventually gave us Black History Month) were attending and graduating from the college. Needless to say, the Kentucky General Assembly was greatly unnerved by Berea's practice of accepting both Black and White students, who were known to take classes together, study together, and even, God help us, date each other. By 1904, the legislative body was desperate enough to pass a law just for Berea, forcing the college to stop taking students of color until the law was amended in 1950.

Another departure from the stereotype was found in Justice John Marshall Harlan, a tobacco-chewing, bourbon-drinking Kentuckian, who wrote the single dissenting opinion when the rest of the U.S. Supreme Court ruled in the case of Plessy v. Ferguson in 1896. The ruling established a standard of "separate, but equal" accommodations that actually forced African-Americans to wait another sixty years for even a modicum of treatment as full citizens. Harlan was well-known for socializing with Latinos, Black Americans, and Asians, and distinguished himself yet again a decade later, when he rallied the Court in a private session to save the life of a Black man in Chattanooga who had been unfairly convicted of rape and sentenced to die.

In point of fact, Kentucky drafted and passed the first Civil Rights Act in the south in 1966, prohibiting discrimination in employment, public accommodations, and housing. And the state passed one of the very earliest Anti-Lynching Laws in 1913, too, only four years after a newly-formed NAACP started demanding them, but my mother remembers lynchings in Clay County up until we moved in 1950, and, it must be remembered that the mountain people were often known to make their own rules about such things.

Clay County, Kentucky, where I was born and spent my earliest years, was carved out of the Appalachian Mountains in 1807. It stands perched at 890 feet above sea-level, in an ancient range rubbed soft and green by the sands of time, characterized by roads impassable and "hollers" up which one might not want to go. To this day, it has less than 22,000 inhabitants in the whole county and most of them are the descendants of people that moved there when the county was new. With forty percent of its residents living below the Federal Poverty Guideline, it has been statistically identified as one of the poorest and unhealthiest counties in the nation. And Black people make up only 4.8% of the population. It wasn't always so. In 1840, with slavery in its heyday, 15% of Clay Countians were African-American. And even in 1850, with a total overall population of less than 5,500, Clay County still sported approximately 550 Black inhabitants, though, of course, 515 were not free to leave.

Named for General Green Clay, a legislator and cousin of Henry Clay, an even more prominent politician of the day, Clay County rapidly took position under the direction of my great-great-great-great-grandfather Hugh White and his brother, James, as one of the leading salt-producing areas in the country. At the time, a lack of refrigeration meant a desperate need for salt to preserve enough meat to feed a nation bursting at the seams. Daniel Boone even offered to re-route the Wilderness Road to pass right by Grandpa's salt works on Goose Creek, but he did not get legislative approval. So, for many years, Uncle James lived, they say, on horseback, conducting his business, back and forth, between Clay County and his plantation in Abingdon, Virginia, and using waterways to branch down to Huntsville, Alabama, where he established such a name for himself that Huntsville's ritziest neighborhood is still filled with things labeled "Whitesburg" in honor of "The Salt King."

I got lost for a couple of months examining books and articles written on what the rest of the world calls "feuds," but what mountain people call "wars." Apparently, my ancestors, the Whites, were deeply implicated in these actions, bullying their way around like the tribal Scotch-Irish highland warriors from which they were descended. It was impossible not to be fascinated by the way they took care of what they simply perceived as their "duty," making sure that people from other families "showed respect" and routinely resorting to the use of guns — and even ambush — to do it. I was reminded of movies like "Menace 2 Society," that portray young Black men being deftly introduced to the same way of life and for many of the same reasons.

I thought back to the episode in my own life, when one of my mother's brothers showed up drunk before dawn at our apartment over the newspaper office in Manchester, the county seat, with the intention of killing his wife, who had brought their children to hide from him there. He had, the story goes, told her to meet him at the railway station and she, inappropriately by mountain standards for women, had disrespected him by ignoring his directive. Children under five scattered like cockroaches as multiple bullets, shot in rapid succession, careened around the room. My five-foot, two-inch mother, in cotton pajamas, fought with him over the gun *mano a mano* as if she were a warrior herself, blood running down her arm from where the hammer kept coming down on the flesh between the thumb and forefinger on her right hand. I always saw my Uncle J.D., who was a lawyer and eventually became a judge, as a hero after that because he came running to take control of his brother. But, in retrospect, it was my *mother* who was the hero. Without her valiant and selfless act of bravery, my aunt — and who knows how many of the rest of us — might have died that morning in a bloody massacre, as a result of rage or accident.

Actually, I recall quite well that my uncles often wore guns in holsters on both hips like cowboys. Being so used to it, I don't remember thinking it at all odd, though my mother worked hard to keep the kids protected from guns lying around the house. And it was, in fact, her concern with how "everybody was their own law" that made her decide to urge my father to take our small family out of the mountains permanently when I was only five-years-old or so. A card game, a car accident killing a pig, or a dispute over a dollar speeding ticket could — and often did — turn into shoot-outs at a moment's notice, with no seeming recourse or negotiation available. It's no wonder I begged for a cowboy suit for Christmas the year I was four and then insisted on wearing it to Sunday School. It gave me the first and only set of guns I ever owned!

Reading about how members of our family would get themselves elected to one office or another as a way of ensuring that they could not be prosecuted for forcing their will or exacting their revenge left me breathless. Referred to as the "Corsica of America," Clay County's reputation was known far and wide. "More money [is] invested in shooting irons than in agricultural instruments," one article proclaimed[ii]. "The Whites have control of the courts and run things as they wish."[iii] As lately as 1986, a story on the front page of the Wall Street Journal described practices of jury-tampering (called "knowing the jury" in Clay County) that resulted in locals not being brought to justice for bombings, sniper attacks, and even unsolved murders.[iv]

Story after story, I read about instances between 1840 and 1932 when the ground ran red with blood; when small armies of feuders would entrench themselves with Winchesters on either side of the courthouse where I eventually played on the grass as a child;[v] when a hundred troops with full support and a Gatling gun would be sent by the Governor, only to have most of them desert in terror before reaching their destination.[vi] It was no wonder that the state decision-makers kept calling for the county to be divided up once and for all among the counties surrounding it. The weirdest part for me was reading how the whole thing, decade after decade, was a stand-off between the two sides of my mother's family, the Whites and the Garrards. It seemed to me that these two families, that inter-married almost as if there were no other choices available, should have been able to work it all out over punch at a wedding reception. But that's not how clans work.

The media took the easy way out and blamed it all on ignorance and isolation. The way the "feuders" were painted in print, you would think they were barely literate and had never been out of the mountains. But in reality, not to say that this was true of all Clay Countians, virtually all of the men in both of my mother's ancestral families were not only college-educated, but lawyers. There were among them judges, county clerks, sheriffs, tax assessors, magistrates, school board commissioners, legislators (both state and federal), a Speaker of the U.S. House of Representatives and, even a Governor. Yet a number of them picked up a gun — and used it, from all accounts — or saw to it that somebody else did.

Women and children were also expected to be involved in many ways to assist their "men-folk," even under fire. It seemed to me that it was overly romantic to think that such viciousness could be based on some 18th century Saxon and Celtic conception of "honor," but the ignorance-and-isolation hypothesis obviously didn't hold either, so I was left shaking my head in confusion and I hadn't even begun to consider the question of slave-holding as yet.

My great-great-grandfather, John E. White, for one, had a notch in his gun by the time he was nineteen-years-old and, over the years, had at least two and maybe three other murders attributed to him directly, though he was never convicted of anything. He was, nevertheless, eventually outdrawn and shot in a bar arguing over a difference of political opinion, which was, after all, the kind of resolution he apparently understood. It is said that this particular incident, however, convinced him to subsequently leave the liquor alone, which would have been difficult for a man in the White family, since the Whites made their own and many of them shared a penchant for rampant drunkenness. With all the blood, guts, and bravado, Clay County history — and my family history with it — read like a Hollywood script for a Grade B western, but with everybody changing hats so fast, you couldn't tell who to root for.

I ultimately had to pull myself away from the topic, though, as it became apparent that those who fought in the Clay County wars were not the only ones in which I was interested. I had to go back farther and deeper to get at the slavery issue. If Great-Great-Great-Great-Uncle James was on horseback all the time, and Great-Great-Great-Great-Grandpa Hugh lived on a creek, what did the slaves do, I wondered. Images of plantation life as I had always imagined it were preventing me from getting the picture.

Then, contacting Dwight Billings to see if he had more specific information, I was informed that he and Kathleen Blee had published a book in 2000 entitled The Road to Poverty: the Making of Wealth and Hardship in Appalachia,[vii] and that they had included an entire chapter on the dynamics of race in Clay County. I harangued local librarians until I could locate a copy that very day. And there it was in all its shining glory: a detailed account of precisely how my ancestors — the slaveholders — had lived. Using this book as a springboard, then, over the several months following, I managed to slowly piece together the best version of the truth I could.

Hugh Lowry White's father moved his household from Pennsylvania to Virginia in 1790 because Pennsylvania had decided to emancipate its slaves that year and, apparently, old William White had no intention of letting that happen to *his* household. It's quite possible, interestingly enough, although there are conflicting stories about this, that old William himself came to the colonies as an indentured servant chased out of Ireland by the British, when the

Scotch-Irish lost their take-over attempt. So it would seem on the surface odd that he had become so heartless so rapidly after arriving, but that he had slaves, we know, and that he moved to Virginia, we know, and unfortunately, that's the kind of information I was often stuck with — bare-bones facts with no explanation for or apparent connection between any of them.

William's son, James, was a master businessman who quickly distinguished himself as a representative for somebody else's entrepreneurial endeavor, and then struck out on his own to seek his fortune, which he fairly quickly began to find. Hearing about the salt wells in the region that eventually became Clay County, Kentucky, James convinced his brother, Hugh Lowry White, who had not amassed his own fortune as yet, to move there in 1803 and oversee a salt manufacturing business for the two of them. They began buying up land in the mountains at a price intended to encourage the development of the area, and by 1840, Hugh was the richest individual in the county, owning $88,000 worth of land and holding $105,400 in personal property — including 38 slaves.

By 1850, the White family interests were producing 250,000 bushels of salt annually and selling them for anywhere from $1 to $5 each. To do this required a great deal of highly dangerous, back-breaking labor and this labor was done by slaves — 162 of them in 1850, mostly men, who were held in bondage by eight households and represented approximately one-third of the total slave population in Clay County. In addition to the slaves they held personally, the Whites rented other slave-holders' slaves, as well, some from as far away as Tennessee, for a yearly amount of $50 to $150 (paid to the slave-holder), but some slave-holders, in the interest of not losing their "property" inadvertently, would contract that their particular slaves could not be used to do the most dangerous types of work.

Slaves drilled salt wells, dug coal, cut timber for fuel, tended furnaces and boiling salt kettles, constructed barrels; built, loaded, and piloted boats; grew crops, and raised and slaughtered animals for use and for sale. As many as one hundred wagons of salt in a train could be seen rolling out of Clay County on a routine basis in 1835, each one pulled by six horses or three yoke of oxen. Even as the Civil War was beginning in 1861, and the death knell for slavery had been sounded, the Whites still held 110 slaves worth $129,935.

As industrial slaves rather than domestic slaves, the African-Americans held by the White family in Clay County lived in what amounted to slave communities, typically crowded into a row of small shacks behind their "master's" house. The seventy-one slaves held by Hugh's sons James and Daugherty White, for example, lived nine to a shanty. And those involved in industry were much more likely to have their lives disrupted by being sold or having their loved ones sold than those serving in other ways.[viii]

According to Billings and Blee,

"...*Clay County's county seat, Manchester, was a bustling slave marketing center. Here, slave traders, salt manufacturers, and farmers crowded around an auction block from which slave men, women, and children were bought, sold, and leased. One former slave remembered seeing lines of slaves standing on an outdoor elevated wooden platform erected in the city center while an auctioneer gave 'a general description of [their] ability and physical standing' and traders beat them with long whips 'to see if*

they could jump around and wuz strong.'"
(p.211)[ix]

Henry Lucas, who served the Whites as an overseer, reported that the slaves liked James, but did not like Daugh, who used to get on a stump when he whipped them. Nevertheless, in 1937, Mrs. Amelia Jones, a former slave living at the time in London, Kentucky, just a few miles west of Manchester, was quoted as saying:

> *"...I was born eighty-eight years ago in Manchester, Kentucky, under a master by the name of Daw White. He was a southern Republican and was elected as congressman by that party...He was the son of Hugh White, the original founder of Whitesburg...*
>
> *"Master White was good to the slaves. He fed us well and had good places for us to sleep, and didn't whip us only when it was necessary, but didn't hesitate to sell any of his slaves. He said, 'You all belong to me and if you don't like it, I'll put you in my pocket,' meaning, of course, that he would sell that slave and put the money in his pocket.*
>
> *"The day he was to sell the children from their mother, he would tell the mother to go to some other place to do some work and, in her absence, he would sell the children. It was the same when he would sell a man's wife. He also sent him to another job and when he returned, his wife would be gone. The master would only say, 'Don't worry. You can get another one.'"[x]*

According to Mrs. Jones, in separate incidences, she lost both her father and her twelve-year-old sister to the auction block, after which they were handcuffed and marched away to southern plantations. Though she said she had enough to eat, Mrs. Jones reported that she had no privileges, and that most masters in Clay County treated their slaves cruelly, underfeeding them and beating them often. The fact that she didn't call separating families from each other without warning a cruel act, even seventy-two years after her ordeal was over, is a testimony to the internalized socialization of oppression, embedded so deeply in the consciousness of the oppressed that it's often there forever. One can only imagine what Mrs. Jones would have described as a cause that would make a whipping "necessary." And, of course, she failed to mention — or was not quoted as mentioning — the other common practice among slaveholders of raping their "property" to produce more of it.

Records indicate that Hugh's son, James, named for his illustrious uncle, not only had a total of twelve children by two successive wives, but routinely had children by his slaves, as well. In 1858, for example, two of James' slaves presented him with babies on the same day, while James was in his fifties and his wife was *also* pregnant! One of his brother Daugh's sons was so dark, it's said that his nickname was "Nig." Even among the broader population of White, free Black and mulatto families, the White family was often implicated in complicated genetic patterns, which are now almost impossible to trace, other than by what is left of oral histories, because they often gave the children last names other than their own. In one case, a mulatto woman was forced to sign a legal paper promising that she would make no legal claim to a child she had birthed to one of the White family members, but the child was not even named in the document, leaving no future record of his or her identity, existence, or whereabouts.

In fact, when the Civil War was over and slaves throughout the South were mandated to appear at courthouses to report their birth years and parents' names in the attempt to create records of them as citizens, no such records were ever collected in Clay County. One cannot assume why this was so, but since members of the White family were often in positions of decision-making authority related to matters of the court, it would not be hard to imagine that they simply did not feel that making official records of paternity among the former slaves would serve the best interests of their reputations. A great deal of money, a great deal of power, a fixation on honor, and a willingness to bury secrets can typically produce such scenarios as appear to have been common in Clay County among the White family for the better part of a century in the 1800s. Then, in 1936, the County Courthouse in Manchester burned down, sealing forever any possibility of tracing the information the White family had guarded so carefully.

African-Americans who were emancipated in Kentucky during the years before the War were not in much better shape than those who were still in bondage. They could be snatched by bounty-hunters, taken south, and enslaved or re-enslaved, regardless of their being free when taken. Their children — as young as two-years-old — could be arbitrarily seized by the courts and forced into "apprenticeships" in service to White families, just because their own families were poor. And they had to carry papers attesting to their status, observe curfews, be gainfully employed or go to jail, and, in general, be very, very careful all the time not to upset anyone who looked White.

Thinking back to my own experiences a hundred years later in the town of Manchester, a town where I could and did, as a three-year-old, walk anywhere alone and without fear, I realize now that the safety I enjoyed was completely attributable to my heritage and my name, though I would have had no way of understanding that at the time. I remember one incident when an African-American man had reached out to me in what was unquestionably, I think now, with all I know, a friendly greeting. I panicked, being very young, and ran from the stranger, who must, then, have panicked himself. I still recall us racing down the street full-tilt, me bellowing at the top of my lungs and him trying frantically to allay my fears by reaching out his arms and calling out to me over and over, "I wouldn't hurt you! I wouldn't hurt you!" I was terrified, but under the circumstances, in 1950 in Clay County, Kentucky, he must have been *twice* as afraid as I was. I wonder if he was subsequently accosted in some way for that unfortunate situation over which he had absolutely no control.

When the Civil War came, my ancestors heard the call and, as they had in the Revolutionary War and against the Native Americans who were, after all, only trying to protect themselves from intruders, the Whites and the Garrards donned uniforms and joined the fight. As individual family members made their choices, each family found itself with members on the side of the Union and the Confederacy both, creating yet again controversy and drama within and among the relatives.

Col. Daniel Garrard's house was said to be the regular information depot for the rebel army in Clay County, but his son, Theophilis Toulmin Garrard (better known as T.T.) fought for the North. Nevertheless, demonstrating the conflicted loyalties of the time and place, T.T. was quoted as saying at one point after the Emancipation Proclamation, "If I'd known Lincoln was going to free the slaves, I'd have fought for the Confederacy instead of the Union."

As if there wasn't already enough animosity between the two branches of the family, the federal government decided that, since it couldn't seem to keep the Confederate forces from accessing the salt wells, it would simply destroy them. So, according to a sign that stands 2-1/2 miles south of Manchester today,

> *"On Oct. 23, 1862, 22nd U.S.A. Brig. including 1st, 2nd, and 20th Ky. Infantry moved here in wake of retreating C.S.A. forces. 500 men worked 36 hours to destroy salt works mainly owned by unionists, but used by Confederates. Loyal U.S.A. citizens were allowed to remove salt enough for their own needs on taking oath none of it would be used to benefit the Confederacy."*

James White wept, saying, "I am ruined for the Union."

But, while cannon balls were driven into the ground to staunch the flow of salt water at the White's Goose Creek Salt Furnace and other White family wells, these locations could eventually be re-opened. The Garrards, on the other hand, with their overall leaning toward the Confederacy, had their well-heads blown up, rendering them permanently useless. Needless to say, this increased and broadened the enmity between the two families.

But there was always something creating havoc between them anyway. For example, in 1859, when my great-great-grandfather John E. White went up to Owsley County and eloped at the age of twenty-one with Elizabeth Garrard Brawner, Col. Daniel Garrard's seventeen-year-old granddaughter, all hell broke loose. The couple had to ride hard by horseback one hundred twenty-five miles, it's said, stopping only for meals and a change of horses. Then they were married in Tazwell, Tennessee, before they could be stopped.

As dramatic as all of this sounds, however, and Grandpa John Ed, as he was called, was a pretty dramatic guy, already known for his hot temper and his love of whiskey, not to mention his reputed murder two years earlier of a Garrard-supported jailor, none of these stories held a candle to the one I came across and then couldn't follow up on. According to John Ed Pearce in <u>Days of Darkness</u>, about the feuds in Clay County[xi],

> *"...On March 1, 1859, Dillon (or Dillion) Hollin was born to a mulatto woman of that name. Everyone knew, and the principals did not deny, that John Ed [White] was the father. Their back-door romance had been going on for some time, and John Ed wanted to marry her, but the Whites begged, threatened, and raised so much trouble that John Ed gave up the idea, though he admitted paternity and supported Dillion." (p. 127)*

I had originally heard about Dillon Taylor White Hollin from a distant cousin, who had done a great deal of tracking of the White and Garrard genealogical information. When I responded with some excitement, he was quick to suggest that the term "mulatto" could mean any mixture of blood lines.

"Oh, no," I corrected him. "According to the dictionary, mulatto only means half Black, half White."

"But Dillon's granddaughter has blond hair and blue eyes," he countered.

"Well, she may have blond hair and blue eyes," I wrote back, "but her Granddad was Black, just the same."

After months of chasing the story, I learned little more than I had known at the beginning. And John Ed's bi-racial child was born only one month before he eloped with Elizabeth. I don't know why John Ed married Elizabeth so quickly after Dillon's birth, if as Pearce suggests, he was in love with Dillon's mother, so we just have to surmise things. Like, well, maybe he was so hurt by not being able to be with Dillon's mother and his son that he went sideways into another relationship. But why a Garrard? Maybe Elizabeth, who was, after all, a real looker, was his second choice. Or maybe he wasn't really in love with Dillon's mother. Or maybe, since they had talked him out of doing what he really wanted to do — based, I'm sure, on family "honor" — he just wanted to piss everybody off and make years more trouble in the family by snatching the granddaughter of a former Governor of the state.

Regardless, he got Elizabeth pregnant almost immediately, and had a son with her the following year. But the boy, named Benjamin Franklin White after his grandfather, died only a few years old, and though John Ed and Elizabeth stayed married for more than fifty years, they only had two more children — in 1862 and 1865 — in spite of the local and family practice of having many. One family account I eventually saw mentioned delicately that Elizabeth was reputed to be "cold" toward her husband throughout their marriage, though the way it began would suggest it didn't start that way.

The family tells the story that Lizzie raised Dillon like he was her own, but the census in 1870 does not list the boy — who would have been ten or eleven-years-old at the time — in John Ed's house. John Ed did send Dillon to the University of Kentucky eventually, as he probably promised Dillon's mother he would, though Dillon only attended for a year until the feuds intensified and he came home to stand beside his father, along with his younger half-brother, my great-grandfather, Daugherty White, named for his slave-holding uncle.

Dillon never owned any land, but he is shown in the 1880 census, at the age of twenty-one, living with a housekeeper right next door to John Ed and Elizabeth. Four years later, he married Sallie Allen, the daughter of a Baptist minister, and before it was over, they had had eight children in a span of fifteen years.

As I thought it over more and more, and put together different pieces of research, I realized that, since Kentucky had slaves until 1865 and had ordered free Blacks out of the state in 1851, then a mulatto woman in Clay County, Kentucky, in 1859, when Dillon was born, was probably either a slave or in the state illegally. There appears to be no birth certificate for Dillon. And no one in the family seems to know his mother's name. Even Dillon's granddaughter assured me that her mother did not know her own grandmother's name, which is highly unusual in Clay County. It is as if the woman did not exist, except that she left a son, my Great-Great-Uncle Dillon, who was shot to death on Christmas eve in 1900 at the age of forty-one while trying to force his daughter to leave a dance.

Dillon's murderers, who were drunk and supposedly feuders from the Garrard side of the conflict, apparently didn't believe that his status as a member of the White family would mean anything because he was born out of wedlock, despite the fact that he was a favorite of his father's. Nevertheless, Dillon's wife Sallie, knowing that everyone would expect her sons to retaliate according to feud law and tradition, was scared that someone would try to kill them before they could act, so John Ed helped her to move the whole household to a different county. Then, for whatever reason, the White family chose not to seek revenge, not to report the crime to the authorities (although everyone knew the four men who had committed the murder), and not to file probate on Dillon's estate until several years later.

Some think it's because, by 1900, the White family dynasty was on the down-hill slide. The freeing of their slaves had cost them dearly, with no way of recouping their losses, since the federal government refused to pay the injury allotments the family felt they deserved because they had backed the Union. And then huge salt domes were discovered farther west and on the Kanawha River in West Virginia, forcing the Whites out of the salt business completely by 1885.

One of the ways White people, such as my family, have avoided feeling responsible for their transgressions against their fellow human beings is simply not to "know" what happened, not to talk about the truth, to "go to the grave," as they say, with secret after secret.

"They held slaves?" they might ask.

"I don't know..." they might add.

"You know, everybody back then..." they try to argue.

"Not *everybody*..." you remind.

"Yeah, well...I don't know..." and they trail off. "That was a *long time ago*."

And it was. But long time ago or not, it happened and it had an effect — on the individuals involved, either master or slave; on the families involved, either master or slave; on the mountain community and the state and the nation in which it stood, to the present.

Zen Buddhists believe that our ancestors are not just pictures in a scrapbook or vaporous memories wafting through time and space in some vacuous manner irrelevant to us, but rather reside yet in the very cells of our bodies, come down through us genetically, for good or ill. As I did my research, reading and poring and thinking and considering, talking to strangers, and reading and poring some more, I began to feel as if they were all around me: old Hugh Lowry and all his sons and grandsons, Col. Daniel and his kith and kin, those who murdered and were murdered, and always and ever, the slaves, listed nameless on slave schedules census after census, distinguished only by their gender, their age, and the name of the one who held them in bondage that year. And, as the days and weeks turned into months, increasingly I saw *her* there, as well: Dillon White Hollin's mother, off to one side, waiting now for one hundred fifty-three years to be granted the right to her name.

After meditating one day, assuring my ancestors that I knew they did the best they could with whatever their consciousness was at the time, that I was forgiving them their drunkenness, their meanness and their cruel self-centeredness, that I was not angry at them for doing awful things and leaving the legacy in my physical, psychological, emotional, and spiritual being, it hit me. They had kept coming to life, generation after generation, until I could be born and write this book. *They wanted the record told.* They knew now that their actions had not served them well, but rather had put a blot on themselves and their progeny that they could not do anything about because they had lived and died without ever acknowledging that all humans are just doing the best they can and that no humans deserve to suffer at the hands of any others.

"Well, that's a bit lofty, isn't it?" my rational mind asserted. "Not to mention convenient, at this late date."

But a few days later, following a thread to something else entirely, I saw it: a little remembrance at the tail-end of a slave narrative I shouldn't even have come across, offered by a woman who had not even been held by the White family:

"My master wuzn't as mean as most masters," reported Sophia Word in 1936 at the age of ninety-nine[xii]. "*Hugh*

White was so mean to his slaves that I know of two gals that killt themselfs. One nigger gal, Sudie, wuz found across the bed with a pen knife in her hand. He whipped another nigger gal 'most to death fer fergitting to put onions in the stew. The next day, she went down to the river, and fer nine days they searched fer her. And her body finally washed up on the shore. The master could never live in that house again as, when he would go to sleep, he would see the nigger standing over his bed. Then he moved to Richmond and there he stayed until a little later, when he hung himself."

Appealing to various sources, I tried to find out whether there was a corroborating family tale among the Whites, but it was not uncommon for a given nuclear family in Clay County to have many children, naming them every one for one or more relatives. My great-great-great-great-grandfather Hugh, for example, had thirteen children, eight of them sons. And, as lately as my mother's generation, there were among her and her seven siblings no less than ten names still carrying on the tradition, including Daugherty, Lowry, and Hugh.

With multiple Hugh Whites holding slaves, then, I wasn't able to identify the particular ancestor or "prove" the account, though I did learn that there was a family home in Richmond, Kentucky. Still, there's no doubt in my mind that the story is true. I can feel it my bones. I can hear it in the whispering wind rustling the leaves on the tree outside my window. But rather than feeling ugly or sad, the feeling is one of resignation and release. A sigh, if you will, that the truth will be told, with or without the details, that the pain he caused others and then his family can be laid to rest in the pages of this book, that the pain that drove him to give up his life will be washed in the light of an old woman's words come to us through history like a song of freedom for us all. We cannot and do not avoid the repercussions of our actions, however ill-guided, socially-accepted, or oblivious.

When I asked my mother about what it was like for her growing up in Clay County as a child, related to the matters at hand, her memories were few. She remembers growing up with African-American "squatters" on her father's land, sharing holidays with them, having them help to get her family through the Great Depression, and not much else.

But one of her memories that I found particularly interesting was that my grandfather, Rob Roy White, her father, would not allow his children to use the "n-word," even in their home, though it was common custom in Clay County to do so. I couldn't help but wonder if his stance had anything to do with the fact that *his* father was raised with a Black half-brother. I know my grandfather was trained as a lawyer, although he never took the bar exam. I know he was an engineer and newspaper editor and sheriff and historian and that he preached the Sunday sermon when there wasn't a preacher in town and that he told Uncle Remus stories using his deep, deep voice in what I recall as perfect Black dialect. But I wish I had known to ask him what he knew about his Uncle Dillon, who died when Pa, as we called him, was already twelve-years-old. Did he know that Dillon was, by every interpretation of the "one-drop" rule, *himself* one of those people that other White people called by that pejorative term? Did he ever hear him called that? Is *that* why he grew up, the grandson of a slaveholder's son, with such strong principles against it?

When I first told Morgan that I wanted this book to make a statement about the socially-constructed, political notion of "race" and relate it to my family's history as slaveholders, she was her usual blunt self in her unhesitating response.

"What do you mean, a *statement*?" she asked flatly.

"I'm not sure," I waffled. "I just want to go on record, as a representative of the White family, accepting responsibility for our past history as...I don't know...some kind of apology, I guess."

"Well, I can tell you one thing," she finished with a flip of her head. "No amount of bullshit liberal White guilt trying to make apologies will *ever* be enough!"

Needless to say, in spite of the fact that I'm pretty used to her nonchalant dismissals when she feels strongly about something, I was a bit taken aback. Not because I didn't agree with her, but because I did. It's not like I was voted the Chairperson of the Whites of Clay County or something. Who did I think I *was* anyway? And after the Civil War, with slavery no longer legal and salt production moved to more centrally located and even more plentiful sources, my ancestors began to live a lot more like ordinary folks.

Besides, despite the fact that Great-Great-Great-Great Uncle James left millions of dollars when he died, his granddaughter Bessie bequeathed it all to her White maid's illegitimate daughter, who was in and out of mental hospitals most of her life and finally died, leaving the money to — of all people — her *lawyer*. It seemed somehow poetic in the face of the White family's use and abuse of that occupation themselves over the years, especially since the base of much of that wealth was ill-gotten through the suffering of others. I had never heard anything about that branch of the family before, so hearing the story now seemed anti-climactic.

Still, money or no, if Morgan was right and I believed that she was, then it wouldn't be enough to just make a polite apology and go on with my life, or even to imagine the book as an effort to make a difference in a racist society in a new millennium, which it is. I had to *do* something. But what?

It didn't take long for the idea to come. I would set up a scholarship, using half of my book royalties, for anyone who could document, using any mechanism whatsoever, that they are descended from a slave who was held by my ancestors. It wouldn't be much. It wouldn't be enough, in any case. But it would be something. It would model for other White Americans that, because we have benefited personally — psychologically, emotionally, and financially — from the exploitation and suffering of Black Americans, we have no choice but to make personal attempts to, at least figuratively, even the playing field ourselves.

I wasn't born with a silver spoon in my mouth, God knows. I remember well using outdoor toilets, taking baths in a sink, and only eating meat for Sunday dinner. But my life and my opportunities from *day one* were prescribed by not only my skin tone, as a White woman, but by the on-going legacy of my position as a member of a family that chose to benefit in a thousand ways by holding other human beings in bondage. Even the way I carry myself these long, long distant days after my family was rich has served me well whenever I wanted it to. I cannot go back and undo even one sad fact of that sad, sad history. But, having looked into my soul and found my ancestors there, I must now let them tell me what they would have me do to stop the on-going saga of our participation in the racism that belongs to all White Americans, no matter what their names.

We are often given to saying in one context or another that two hundred fifty years of slavery has had an on-going effect on the African-American community in the United States. What we don't say, largely because no one has forced us to, is that two hundred fifty years of being *slaveholders* has had an on-going effect on *us* — the White American community, even for those individuals and families that never held a slave themselves.

Very few White Americans ever made — before or after the Civil War — the kind of sacrifices necessary to hold themselves outside the racist construct that our social institutions were established to be from the outset. The rest of us — all the rest of us — have been complicit by our lack of protest, complicit by our participation in the institutional oppression that has *always* given us the most of the best and the least of the worst, complicit by our ready acceptance of the economic prosperity that was produced for us *as a nation* by millions of Black laborers working twelve to fifteen-hour days for free year after year after year for two and one-half centuries.

My ancestors called themselves Christian people, if you examine the records or even ask the family today. And it's hard for White people to understand, admit, or deal with the reality that being "Christian" by category (rather than "Christ-like" by principle and practice) has never precluded individuals and groups from being less than moral or even from committing atrocities. The Crusades and the Inquisition stand as ready proof of that.

Montesquieu's assertion in <u>The Spirit of the Laws</u>[xiii] that Blacks had no souls laid the groundwork for a raft of "Christian" nations to unleash fleet after fleet of slave ships, killing millions of Africans horrifically to fill endless coffers with gold. Even once that perspective was discarded, many Whites purported that it was better to enslave and convert Africans to Christianity, however brutally it was accomplished, than to leave them to die as free people in "heathen" lifestyles of their own choice and tradition.

All of our nation's "founding fathers" were slaveholders, even as they claimed that God had created all men equal. Further, the churches themselves in the southern states held tens of thousands of slaves before the Civil War for the purpose of renting them out[xiv]. And slaveholders, including my ancestors, I'm sure, appear to have thought nothing of going to church on Sunday, having beaten a slave half to death and rubbed salt in his or her wounds the day before for not having worked fast enough or some other offense deemed punishable without conscience.

Even a century later, Christian believers often seem able to skirt issues that would seem on the surface to call into question the morality of their faith when it intersects with "race." Where were the Christian ministers *after* the Rev. Martin Luther King, Jr., wrote his letter from the Birmingham jail challenging them to support African-Americans as they suffered for daring to suggest that they, too, were children of God and equal to White folks? Where is the protest in the Christian community when the Ku Klux Klan burns crosses as the symbol of their belief-system or wears crosses on their robes while espousing their poisonous doctrines *today*? Where is the organized response from Christians when the Christian Identity movement and other so-called religious entities tout beliefs that pair rabid White Supremacy with fundamentalist Christian dogma? The routine practice of overt, covert, and subtle racism by well-meaning White people who profess Christianity would make the Jesus who threw the money-changers' tables out of the temple go ballistic all over again. "We have met the enemy," said Charlie Brown once years ago in the popular cartoon, Peanuts, "and it is *us*." Indeed. And we don't want to hear it.

Too many of us ignore the jokes, minimize what African-Americans tell us about their experience of life, *always* think we got the job because we deserved it, *always* assume that a Black person got hired because somebody *had* to hire them, walk on eggshells around racist family members so as not to "offend" them, date and marry racists (not considering it to be a fatal flaw), and don't reach out to make a real difference because we're too busy, too uncomfortable, too unclear about what exactly to do, too few, and too...racist?

So many White people are so conflicted over the socially-constructed, political notion of "race," we have convinced ourselves that the nearly 800 active hate sites on the internet[xv] viciously hyping the murder and degradation of Black people are *really* just exercising their First Amendment rights. So there are laws against speeding and under-age drinking, but hate-mongering against people of color is "constitutional" in the United States. "Inciting to *riot*" is illegal; inciting to *murder* is not. *Paying* someone to kill is illegal, but psyching people up to kill people of color for *free* is protected by U.S. *law*.

This idea also manifests itself through extra-judicial executions by law enforcement officers who killed on average in 2015 a Black man, woman, or child every twenty-eight hours[xvi]. These incidents often involve what turns out to be fabricated or "lost" evidence and cover-ups at every level of authority, followed by an absolute lack of apology or accountability of any kind. The flat-faced shrugs with which Black family anguish is typically met in these cases resulted in 2014 in the founding of the Black Lives Matter movement. Yet even that presentation of outrage was countered almost immediately by a vehemently defensive All Lives Matter movement claiming that Black people deserve no more compassion than anyone else which missed the point entirely that Black people in the United States, in fact, routinely receive far *less* compassion – or even protection – than White citizens.

The White Supremacist mind-set with which we are socialized from birth makes it possible for Black people to continue to be relegated to the back of the social bus and then blamed for being there. We know there are many indigent White people in this country, but where the pockets of poverty are the most long-standing and the most egregious, the faces tend to be Black and the most widely accepted theories about why this is so are rooted in the White Supremacy that birthed this reality in the first place.

Schools where the students are disproportionately Black are invariably underfunded and over-disciplined, so children learn early and well that they are not expected, encouraged, or prepared to advance. Those that manage to do so anyway are used as an excuse to continue to underserve them all. And the pipeline-to-prison trajectory[xvii] that so many Black male youths are tracked onto as young as elementary school guarantees that they will not subsequently be able to compete for scholarships, jobs, housing, or any of the other benefits of living a "better" life.

In short, African-Americans are systematically prevented from exercising their rights as human beings in the land of their birth. And White people know it. When educator Jane Elliott asks audiences of White people which of them would like to be treated the way Black people are treated in this country, no one makes a peep. Yet they will argue that they deserve the disproportionate benefits they expect to enjoy (whether they ever do or not).

The reality is that all oppressors in history came to believe over time that they were superior to whomever they oppressed. The Egyptians, the Romans, the Ottomans, the British, the Nazis in Germany – all believed they were superior to others when, in fact, they simply had the moral will to commit unmitigated violence to maintain their unbridled power. And all fell. In fact, there has never been a society in the history of the world that went up and never came down. The illusion of superiority is not and will never be permanent because it is a lie. So if pride, indeed, comes before a fall, those who cling to White Supremacy and the illusion of White superiority are damning this nation to its own disastrous finale. And those who hold their silence at this pivotal moment will go down in history as wanting to be on top more than they wanted their nation to survive.

---

[i] Institute for Research on Poverty Discussion Paper No. 1064-95, March 1995.

[ii] The Road to Poverty: the Making of Wealth and Hardship in Appalachia by Dwight Billings and Kathleen Blee (Cambridge University Press, 2000)

[iii] Rev. John Jay Dickey, *Diary*, October 3, 1898.

[iv] Wall Street Journal, February 23, 1986. Pp 1, 23.

[v] London Mountain Echo, June 14, 1898.

[vi] "Face to Face" December 25, 1898, clipping in the Berea Collection, Berea College.; The Road to Poverty: the Making of Wealth and Hardship in Appalachia by Dwight Billings and Kathleen Blee (Cambridge University Press, 2000), p. 288.

[vii] The Road to Poverty: the Making of Wealth and Hardship in Appalachia by Dwight Billings and Kathleen Blee (Cambridge University Press, 2000)

[viii] For a particularly comprehensive -- and sometimes graphic -- description of slave life in Clay Country, Kentucky, see pages 144-156 in Blame It On Salt: The First 150 Years of an Unruly County and Some of Its People by Charles House (Pub This Press, 2007)

[ix] The Road to Poverty: the Making of Wealth and Hardship in Appalachia by Dwight Billings and Kathleen Blee (Cambridge University Press, 2000)

[x] Slave Narratives: A Folk History of Slavery in the United States Taken From Interviews With Former Slaves, Prepared by the Federal Writers Project, 1936-1938. Sponsored by the Library of Congress. www.memory.loc.gov/mss/mesn/070/070.pdf (Pp 38-39)

[xi] Days of Darkness: The Feuds of Eastern Kentucky by John Ed Pearce (The University of Kentucky Press, 1994).

[xii] Slave Narratives: A Folk History of Slavery in the United States Taken From Interviews With Former Slaves, Prepared by the Federal Writers Project, 1936-1938. Sponsored by the Library of Congress. http://memory.loc.gov/mss/mesn/070/070.pdf (Pp 66-68)

[xiii] The Spirit of the Laws by Charles de Secondat, Baron of Montesquieu with the help of Claudine Guerin de Tencin, Bk 15, Ch. 5 (1748)

[xiv] Divided by Faith: Evangelical Religion and the Problem of Race in America by Michael Emerson and Christian Smith (2001)

[xv] Southern Poverty Law Center at www.splcenter.org

[xvi] RT.com, 12/22/15 www.rt.com/usa/326724-police-killings-usa-report ; The Guardian, 12/31/15 www.theguardian.com/us-news/2015/dec/31/the-counted-police-killings-2015-young-black-men

[xvii] "The School-To-Prison Pipeline: Time to Shut It Down" by Mary Ellen Flannery, NEA Today, 1/5/15

EPILOGUE

Four days after I finished my book, after celebrating my birthday with crab-stuffed shrimp and tira misu, I came home to find an e-mail waiting for me from someone I didn't know. I had sent out a blanket request a couple of weeks before on several genealogy list-servs seeking information related to Dillon White Hollin's mother. I was almost done with the book at the time, but had not tried this, as yet, and hoped for a last minute miracle. None came and I had finished the book, assuming that none would.

"I doubt if you will get very many responses to your questions," the unexpected e-mail began. "Dillon is listed in the White family bible. I would be curious to know what information you have to share..." And it was signed "Regards."

I immediately decided that this was my birthday present from the Universe. I figured that I had nothing to lose anyway, so without even waiting until morning, I gratefully and graciously outlined everything I knew, genuflecting appropriately to demonstrate my good faith and respect.

Within thirty-six hours, I had it, at least what there was to have.

My informant, as we call them in sociology, who chose to remain anonymous, had his own reasons for searching out the name of Dillon's mother and, consistent with my earlier struggles, had not found in a decade of rigorous research "absolute proof" available. Nevertheless, he had done much work and had a theory that made sense to me.

It centers around a tiny family listed in the Clay County census in 1860, a little more than a year after Dillon's birth. A Jeff Allen, age 22, and his wife, Mary, age 17, whose marriage was recorded on January 25th of that year, appear in the census with a 2-year-old son listed as "Dilliard Hollandsworth."

It's important to understand that names were apparently changed more or less at will in Clay County in those days and not necessarily in court. A given member of the Hollingsworth family, for example, might also appear variously over time as a Hollinsworth, Hollandsworth, Holland, Hollan, Hollen, or Hollin. Census takers, for one thing, didn't seem concerned with consistency, spelling, or for that matter, any form of documentation on either race or name. Needless to say, this plays havoc with the ability to follow a genealogical thread. But once you accept it as more or less inevitable, any irritation is minimal, though it cannot help but leave one somewhat perplexed. Is it them? Is it not? Who would know? Did they mean to do this and, if so, why? Questions reign supreme and often without any clear answers.

Still, the date and ages seemed plausible. And, though the original Hollingsworth family came into Clay County in the very early 1800's listed as "free whites," whatever that is, most of those with the various versions of their name were subsequently listed as Black or mulatto at one point or another. This is a major issue, since central to the story about Dillon and his mother is always the fact of her race being the reason John Ed was talked out of marrying her. And while the story has been orally transmitted from generation to generation and household to household for a century and a half, that one detail has always remained intact against great resistance from all branches of the White family.

By 1870, when a ten-year-old named "Dillian" appears as a farm worker in the household of James C. White (both of them listed as Black) and another ten-year-old named "Dilliard" appears in the household of an Elizabeth Parker (both of them listed as mulatto), Jeff and Mary had seemingly vaporized, at least out of Clay County. It would appear likely, at least on the surface, that, if Mary was Dillon's mother, then she left him to John Ed's protection, with John Ed's agreement, but not in John Ed's house.

Ten years later, in 1880, a 21-year-old "Dillian Holland" is found in the census immediately next door to John Ed and Lizzie and their two children, Ella and Daugherty. That John Ed wanted Dillon close to him, however this practice grieved his wife, as it must have or Dillon would have been in the White family home, suggests that John Ed *did* more than likely feel very strongly about Dillon's mother, Mary.

There is no way to know at this point, given what little we have as information, whether or not Dillon knew his mother. It is absolutely within the realm of possibility that he did not, since the Whites made an art form out of secrecy, backed up with legal expertise. Still, he may have been told. If John Ed had once loved her as much as it seems that he might have, given his commitment to their son, it's not beyond imagination.

A number of the White family males had many children out of wedlock — slave and free — that they did not claim or acknowledge. There is even some indication that John Ed had at least one other child out of wedlock himself some years after Dillon was born. But only Dillon, to the best of my knowledge, of all the White family members born out of wedlock, was held close and claimed and supported in the way that he was.

So, I was a bit taken aback, actually, when I received a copy of a letter from one elderly Clay Countian to another, describing the murder of Dillon Hollin and making his racial heritage finally, utterly clear. The men who shot my grandfather's uncle that dark night were drunk and dancing until he arrived. Dillon, married to a Baptist minister's daughter, was loathe to have his only daughter, Ada, out dancing at local affairs, especially in the face of his having spent his life having to listen to his mother being maligned for having had him outside of marriage.

Apparently, Ada didn't want to leave the party and her dancing partner, John Lucas, being drunk and a Garrard supporter, decided to use the opportunity to get in a lick against the White family. With the help of several other men, he shot Dillon White Hollin point blank without even going outside to do it, calling Dillon, as he did so, "White's nigger bastard." I wonder if those were the last words my Great-Great-Uncle Dillon ever heard. I wonder if he thought about his mother as they were spat out at him, meant to kill his soul even as the bullets killed his body. And I wonder if Mary Hollinsworth Allen was alive or dead at that moment in time. But regardless, as a mother myself, I'll bet she was there, somehow, arms around her son, in spite of them all.

How different it would all have turned out if Dillon had just let Ada go to the party that night. How different it would all have turned out if Clay County, Kentucky, had not been so violent in those earlier times. How different it would all have turned out if John Ed had married Mary regardless of what the rest of the family said. And how different it would all, all, all have turned out if the socially-constructed political notion of race did not prescribe the lives of all Americans, including my ancestors, my children, and myself.

ABOUT THE AUTHOR

Rebecca Hensley started studying race relations in the United States in 1963 and never figured out how to stop. Along the route, she added to the mix graduate school, rigorous research, a blog she's been writing for ten years, and a bi-racial daughter. She makes no apology for wanting to see racial justice implemented in our White Supremacist nation. And she works to socially-reproduce herself so this mission will go forward whether or not it is accomplished in her lifetime.

Her website can be found at www.rebeccahensley.com, and her blog on race relations (www.WhyAmINotSurprised.blogspot.com) has been visited 450,000 times in nearly 200 countries.

www.ingramcontent.com/pod-product-compliance
Lightning Source LLC
Chambersburg PA
CBHW030427290526
45786CB00001B/171